No More Fear

*"Nation will not take up sword against
nation, nor will they train for war
anymore. Every man will sit under his
own vine and under his own fig tree, and
no one will make them afraid..."*
(Micah 4:3-4)

No More Fear

from Killing Fields to Harvest Fields

Physa
Chanmany

as told to Catherine Lawton

CLADACH
PUBLISHING

ISBN 0-9670386-0-X

10 9 8 7 6 5 4 3 2 1

Acknowledgments

I want to thank the eternal God, my Heavenly Father, who is holy, gracious, and loving. I praise Him for who He is. Thank you Lord Jesus, Lord Holy Spirit, for saving, redeeming, protecting, and preserving my life. You are the Life-Giver before and in the beginning of time. Your name is blessed and holy above all. Amen.

I thank God for my wife Rachelle, who loves and supports me. I thank her for sharing her hopes and dreams with me.

I thank God for all the people whose names have been mentioned in this story, for they were God's help and God's messengers to me.

~~ Rev. Physa Chanmany   (Psalm 36:5-10)

My deep and overflowing thanks go to Jesus Christ, my Lord who stands on life's shore, sending his people forth on the sea of faith to venture for him, while at the same time constantly and mystically welcoming us to his refuge and safe harbor.

My thanks also go to my sister, Bev Coons, and friends Joe and Eloise Powell and Ron and Kathy Lundy who read, critiqued, and encouraged the writing of this book.

Finally, oceans of thanks to my husband Larry, daughter Christina and son David for being my anchor and inspiration in this life.

~~ Catherine Lawton

MAP #1

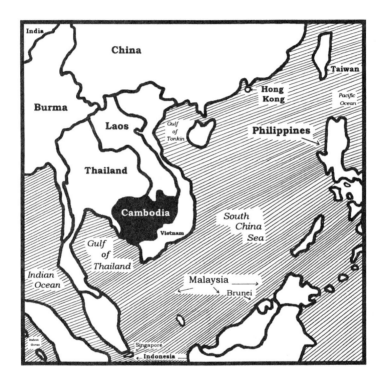

Cambodia in its Southeast Asia setting.

CONTENTS

ILLUSTRATIONS

PREFACE

During my youth in the 1960's and 70's I saw television and magazine pictures of teen-aged Vietnamese and Cambodian soldiers, small, tough, skinny, and lugging big rifles. I didn't imagine that one of those boys would someday be my friend and that I would write his story.

These Vietnam-era media images of guerrillas in Southeast Asian jungles were imprinted in the consciousness of my generation; but we had little understanding of the people groups who inhabited those jungles--their rich history and culture, their way of life, or their desire to know God.

In succeeding decades, as refugees flooded into our country, Christians began to view this situation as a mission field arriving on our doorstep. In the early 1980's, a family of "boat people" literally moved into our home when my husband and I, along with a group of friends from our church, sponsored a Vietnamese refugee family, a short-term involvement. One of our number, Eloise Powell, continued to work with refugees, helping them with language and cultural adjustments. She found the Laotian refugee community particularly receptive. Eloise began to teach these people about God, as revealed in his son, Jesus Christ. She taught Bible lessons to children in the refugee neighborhoods.

These children were bused to Vacation Bible School one summer, and they loved it! They begged their parents to bring them to Sunday School on Sundays. Then Eloise began a Sunday School class for the adults, most of whom are Htin hill-tribe people from Laos.

The class flourished and Eloise needed help. She searched and found--in Modesto, California--an educated Cambodian man who had come to America as a refugee and was now an ordained Christian minister, who spoke the Lao, Khmer, and Thai languages. This man was Physa Chanmany, whose story you now hold in your hands.

Like many Americans, I used to lump together all Southeast Asian people--Vietnamese, Laotian, and Cambodian, etc.. But I am learning how unique each of these people groups is--in history, culture, religion, as well as in national and personal identity.

The uniqueness of Cambodia shines in the accounts of its history. It knew the greatest glory when the Khmer Kingdom of Angkor extended into what is now Thailand, Laos, and Vietnam. This glory is still evident in the spectacular and world-renowned ruins of 9th to 14th century Angkorian temples and palaces.

On the other extreme, Cambodia has been devastated by one of the worst Communist regimes in history. The term "Killing Fields" conjures up reports--still being confirmed--of the genocidal Pol Pot regime which made slaves of an entire nation and tried to wipe out a culture. At the hands of the Khmer Rouge Communists, between 1975 and 1979, nearly two million Cambodians (out of a population of seven million) perished.

According to the U.S. Committee for Refugees, between 1975 and 1995 a total of 147,120 Cambodian refugees were admitted to the United States. These numbers do not include immigrants. (Refugees are granted political asylum on the basis of a "well-founded fear of persecution.") As one refugee has stated, "Immigrants come here

6

looking for a better life. Refugees come here for a life."

One of these coming-here-for-a-life and home-land-less people, Physa Chanmany has known "well-founded fear" and loss; but, finding newness of life in Jesus Christ, he has devoted his life to helping other refugees rebuild their lives centered on a foundation of Christian faith, community, and worship.

I thank God for the privilege of knowing this brother, of glimpsing the awesome hand of God's providence at work in his life, and of helping him to tell his amazing story.

For many hours in Physa's office, I listened while he recounted his experiences--vividly, enthusiastically, even dramatically; while I pictured it all in my mind's eye, jotting scrawls that later shaped into a book-length manuscript.

We often laughed. But some parts of the story were too difficult to relate, some memories too painful to dig up. When Physa became uncharacteristically silent, I knew he had reached a point in his story that best lay unspoken, left covered by the healing balm of Jesus. Physa also hesitated when he saw that the descriptions of his people's sufferings brought tears to my eyes.

To better understand the setting and context of Physa's story, I researched library, internet, and bookstore sources. In the bibliography, I have listed most of these resources for readers who desire to learn more about the history, culture, and Christian outreach in today's Cambodia, as well as among Southeast Asian refugees in America.

Physa's childhood village near the Thai border was destroyed by the Khmer Rouge in their attempt to demolish family life. Khmer Rouge guerrillas have hidden nearby in the jungle for the past twenty years, attacking and raiding. Anti-personnel mines litter forests, fields, and farmland. This is not a place you and I are likely to visit soon. Tourists to Cambodia are advised to limit their travels to south and central Cambodia's main roads to avoid landmines, bullets, and snakes.

But here is your opportunity to visit a village on the edge of tropical forests in northwestern Cambodia, where rice farmers religiously attempted to worship the only gods they knew in order to accumulate merit for an endless cycle of future lives with little hope of escape from sufferings.

Enjoy the visit... Then feel the fear when Khmer Rouge soldiers evacuate villagers to the forced labor camps and killing fields... Later, rejoice to see God's light shine into the darkness... And I hope that you will allow the Lord Jesus to reveal his love to you afresh, and that he will place in your heart a desire to pray for refugee peoples that God will wipe away their tears and defuse their fears.

As we learn to listen to the aliens in our midst, may we hear the voice of God who says, "...my house will be called a house of prayer for all nations." (Isaiah 56:7) May we inclusively and supportively join hands to praise the God who also says, "I will be exalted among the nations," (Psalm 46:10) before we discover that we are the ones who have become the mission field.

Together, we'll sing a new song to the Lamb: "...And with your blood you purchased men for God from every tribe and language and people and nation. You have made them to be a kingdom and priests to serve our God." (Revelation 5:9)

--Catherine Lawton, June 1999

8

PART 1

In the past,
he let all nations go their own way.
Yet he has not left himself
without testimony;
he has shown kindness
by giving you rain from heaven
and crops in their seasons;
he provides you with plenty of food
and fills your hearts with joy.
(Acts. 14:16-17)

1. Jungle Village

People never locked their doors in our village. We had no need for policemen. No fences divided our yards.

I grew up in the village of Kaubtom, in the province of Battambang, in the country of Kampuchea (also called Cambodia), near the border of Thailand.

A river ran through our village, providing life and livelihood. In the center of the village stood the Buddhist temple, surrounded by a park where we had festivals and celebrations. Near the temple stood the quarters for the Buddhist monks and the boys given to them by village families to raise and train. Close by was built the village school.

Radiating from that center, dirt roads and paths meandered outward, past many large, multi-roomed, single-pagoda-roofed houses built high on posts or pillars. Each pillar was made of a whole tree--so large, a child could not reach his arms around it; stripped smooth so termites would not eat it; and often carved artistically. Our house was built on sixteen of

11

these beautiful posts. In the space under the house, we kept the farm animals.

The indefinite boundaries of the sprawling yards were thickly planted with tropical fruit trees and thorny bushes, at intervals cut through to make pathways for walking from yard to yard.

Village men helped each newly-married couple build one of our Thai and Lao style homes, using hand-sawn mahogany from the forest and metal roofing bought in the city.

The roads led past the houses to the plots of farmland owned by each family. People walked about an hour on the road to reach their farms each day. Along the road tropical trees and grasses grew so high that children had to stay on the road to see where they were going. Beyond the farms, lushly foliaged hills rose to mountains and the tall trees made a densely forested jungle. We called the mountain and the jungle, *Phnom-malai.*

The families grew rice, fruits, and vegetables on their small farms. We sold part of the rice crop to rice mills in the city. The nearest small city was a two-hour walk from our village. Many people rode bikes to this town. Few people in our village had cars--only wealthier people connected with businesses, such as rice mills. The large city of Battambang was a two-hour car drive away. But few people went there, since it was a very long walk.

With the money from the sale of our rice, we bought salt, medicine, and clothing--the only things we needed from the city. Otherwise, our village was self-sufficient and rich in natural resources as well as rich in community.

During the rainy season from May to November, when the reddish waters of the river flooded the village and overflowed into the rice paddies, the rice crops and vegetable gardens grew under billowy-clouded, changing skies and we had food in abundance: fish, crabs, snails, and fish eggs. The people ate all these.

The men also hunted in the jungle for large lizards, turtles, deer, jungle fowl, and wild oxen. Many types of edible mushrooms grew in the rich forest floor, in places where the trees grew less thickly and the sunlight shone through the canopy. We gathered edible green plants which we cooked with fish in delicious soup. The forest also yielded a bounty of wild fruit in its season. Everyone shared.

I could not imagine going hungry or starving.

As a child, I would lie in bed listening to the croaking frogs and crying crickets sing their many-toned songs. The frogs always sang before and after the rain, and I felt happy when the rain started tapping out its own rhythmic songs on the metal roof. I fell asleep with anticipation of the morning, knowing that the rain and wind would knock the fruit off the trees in the night. Then in the morning we children hurried outside to find the fresh fallen mangos, guavas, sugar palm fruit, and other tropical fruits that ripened during this season.

Children were not allowed to climb into the trees in other people's yards to pick the fruit; but when it fell on the ground, all the children of the village were free to pick it up and eat it. On those humid, warm mornings we children searched for the juicy fruit to put in our pockets, take home to wash and eat, or carry to school with us as a snack.

I was a school boy. The government of our country, influenced by the French, provided schooling for all children who wanted an education. The government paid teachers from the city to go and teach school in provincial villages like ours. These teachers were strict, punishing us for every infraction or mistake. For school, instead of our traditional clothing, we wore uniforms like all other school children in our country. Boys wore white shirts and blue pants or shorts, and girls wore white blouses and blue skirts.

We didn't have school books. Only the teacher had the government curriculum texts, which they read to us or copied on the blackboard. We had to write down the dictated lesson and memorize it word for word. Once a week students stood before the class to recite.

If a student hadn't memorized the lessons for the week, the teacher told him to stand on one leg for ten or fifteen minutes in front of the class. If he put the other foot down, the teacher switched his leg. The other students snickered at him. Some children didn't want to study and didn't like the discipline. They quit and worked on the family farm. Some parents didn't want their children to go to school and learn. Many families did not send their daughters to school.

"You don't need to learn," parents told their daughters.

"You will be a wife and listen to your husband."

Other kids quit school because they did not pass exams. As the French do, students, no matter what age, were not moved to the next grade unless they passed an exam each year. Older students kept in lower grades were teased.

We learned to read and write the Khmer (Cambodian) language. We learned history, geography, and math. Sometimes we wrote essays, stories, and poetry. We had art lessons, and learned to carve objects out of wood. In the higher grades, students were required to learn French.

I attended school for ten years, and studied hard because I liked to learn and I didn't want to suffer the ridicule of punishment.

The children attended school Monday through Wednesday, and Friday through Saturday. On Thursdays and Sundays we helped with the farm work. I took care of the family's farm oxen and cows.

School started at 7:30 in the morning, so every morning I got up early. I first had to do my chores. I fed the chickens and pigs. I remember watching the chickens. When an eagle flew over, the chicks ran to the mother who covered them with her wings. If a chick didn't run to its mother, the eagle would swoop and snatch it up and I would hear *peep, peep, peep* as the eagle carried the chick off to eat it. I thought nothing could snatch me away from my secure and happy life.

Years later when I learned about God and the Bible, I read Luke 13:34-35 and I remembered those chicks, and I knew that although it can happen that evil powers snatch us away; yet there is a greater, unseen power to whom we can run and find refuge. But these things had not entered my mind as a young village boy, farm boy, and school boy. I thought I would be safe if I stayed close to my mother and to the ways of my elders.

On Saturdays, the school children had competitions in sports and in performing arts, such as singing and acting. I was outgoing and smart and I enjoyed competing in music and drama.

"Tum, you are like your father," my mother told me.

My short, dark-skinned father was a talented amateur singer and actor, often asked to perform at weddings and temple festivals. My father worked as a carpenter and a farmer.

My mother--tall and lighter skinned, strong and determined--was of Lao (Laotian) descent. My father had both Lao and Khmer grandparents. We often spoke the Lao language at home, and we spoke the national language of Khmer at school, in the marketplace, and in the city.

My parents remembered the days, during their youth, when our province of Kampuchea was controlled by neighboring Thailand. The French won Battambang and Siem Reap provinces back from the Thai. During the time of Thai control, the people of my village learned to speak the Thai language, also.

I was the seventh-born of my parents' eight children.

One of my earliest memories is of my number one brother, Boun, who was very intelligent, but who had a rebellious desire to explore. He learned carpentry from our father. When he was nineteen, a business man from the city came to the village selling doors. Boun

18

paid half of our rice to buy six doors for our house. When our mom came home from the farm, she became angry with him. My brother ran away to Laos country, and three of his friends followed him. I was about three years old. I tried to run after Boun. He gave me a letter for Mom, one riel (Khmer money) to buy a lollipop for myself, and he told me to go back.

"Tell Mom I'm taking the bike," he said. It was our only bicycle.

Boun lived in a Buddhist temple in Laos. A rich man worshiped there often. He adopted Boun and hired him to work in his rice mill. Boun married and learned electronics. We didn't hear from him again until many years later, when the war with Vietnam would bring him back to Cambodia as a communist officer.

My number two brother, named Soon, grew up to be a farmer and worked the family farm, and helped our mother.

The next child born, a son, died of a high fever at age three. This is the only child my mother has lost, despite the wars that took many lives.

The next son born, Art, became the number three brother; and he was another adventurer. My mother gave birth to him while she was working in the rice field. The baby fell on a rock, cut his forehead, and to this day he bears a scar. As a young man, Art ran away from home. I considered him my "lost brother" until many years later when I found him in a far-away place unheard of to me as a boy.

The fourth child born was a girl--the jewel of the family. She was named Naiang, meaning "dear".

When Naiang was very small, she nearly choked to death on a fish bone. My parents blamed each other, and they wouldn't stop arguing and accusing each other.

One evening my dad returned home from working on the farm. As was his custom, he bathed and put on a scarf-like sarong tied loosely around his waist. He and my mother began arguing. She grabbed the sarong and pulled if off to shame him. In retaliation, he took hold of the pot of food she was cooking and threw it on the ground.

They began to talk of divorce.

With great concern, all the relatives and other people of the village came together and surrounded my parents. The people talked and talked to my mom and dad, convincing them to be reconciled and stay together.

After that my parents had three more children: another son, named Nonglam, who was a good boy and a good farmer; then in 1960 I was born. My parents named me "Tum", a Lao name meaning "righteous". Last came my little sister, Pheny.

My father died when I was only two or three. I don't remember his face; but I remember watching him fish with nets. And I remember running to meet him when he returned home from the farm in the evenings. He teased me by trying to walk as I held on to his feet. One day he fell asleep with a fever and never awoke. But, living in the house he built, I had the work of his hands by which to remember him. And I had grandparents, uncles, and aunts who lived nearby.

On the wooden floor of our house, all the family sat on hand-woven mats. Men sat cross-legged. Ladies sat with knees to the side and their feet carefully kept out of sight. Young girls and young boys each had a certain acceptable way of sitting. Young people were not allowed to sit in the manner of older people;

neither could boys and girls sit alike. We ate our meals at a wooden table that stood two inches off the floor.

I loved mornings in the dry season when extended families gathered round the fire on cool mornings. Waking before sunrise, when we heard the roosters crow, we children wrapped up in blankets and hurried outside where the adults were cooking breakfast on the fire: sweet potatoes, tata root, and sweet rice wrapped in bamboo skins. Under the stars, we huddled in our blankets near the warmth of the fire, savoring the delicious food. The old grandpas told us the names of the stars. And they told us stories from their childhoods and the Khmer legends of long ago.

They told us about the ancient worship of the evil snake god that had seven heads and controlled the Khmer Kingdom. The god of India came and the two became one, and the Brahmin were born.

The legends said that Kampuchea was cursed by the snake god. Even the word "Kampuchea" in the Khmer language literally means, "Suffering-Healing".

As a carefree boy, I had no idea what degree of suffering, as well as healing, was coming for the people of my peaceful village.

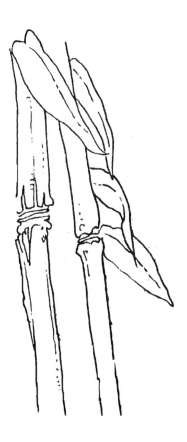

2. Deceived

According to the stories handed down, the people of my village descended from a politically strong tribe of a great warlord hundreds of years ago, when the Khmer and Lao royal families formed alliances, intermarried, and produced the mixed ancestry of my people. This was written in the Chronicles of Laos after King Fa-Ngum. Though the historical record of Southeast Asia tells of continual conflicts between the Khmer people and their Thai and Vietnamese neighbors, not even one story tells of the Lao and Khmer people fighting each other. We always called each other "brother".

Later, when Burmese invaders overcame our Lao-Khmer tribe, instead of submitting to their conquerors and becoming slaves, the forebears of my village people escaped and migrated to the eastern area of present-day Thailand that used to be part of Lao country. Then when the Thai took control of that area, as well as two western provinces of Kampuchea, they migrated to the protective jungle area where I was born and nurtured.

In the no-man's-land jungle of Battambang province, the migrating tribe found food aplenty in the wild vegetation and animal life: wild jungle cattle (called *kouprey*), wood hogs, wild pigs, deer, quail, wild chickens, as well as monkeys and snakes. During the rainy season, when the Tonle Sap lake swelled and flowed back into the rivers, the river where my tribal people started their village overflowed, watering the crops and providing a lavish supply of fish. Each family staked out a piece of land for their house and cleared plots in the forest for their rice paddies and vegetable farms.

These Lao-Khmer people peacefully farmed and became more and more prosperous; the village grew bigger and bigger.

After Vietnamese war started in the east, many pure Kampucheans (who spoke only Khmer) migrated to our village, also.

Some of the people of my village owned jeeps, tractors, motorcycles, and bicycles. My family had a motorcycle and a bicycle. Most people owned radios.

Our village got newspapers from the nearby town. My parents learned the Khmer language from Buddhist monks, so they understood the radio broadcasts and newspapers. They had some awareness of the political unrest and changes in our country: the Kampuchean communist party which was formed before I was born; world powers playing increasing roles in Kampuchea's economy and politics; the building of highways and an airline; technology and factories developing in the city; schools, universities, and the arts growing; imports and exports increasing.

At the same time, in the capital city of Phnom Penh, a prosperous, educated, governing, upper class were breaking from the work ethic of our society, living lives of comfort and leisure, pocketing some of the western aid, making alliances with powerful nations, and taking advantage of poor people. The communists used this situation to arouse resentment and anger in the country people who were joining them.

As I was growing up, increasingly we heard about wars, bombings that were crossing our borders in the east; about unrest in the cities, and demonstrations and attacks against the government by Khmer communists aided by the Chinese. But our people had fought with the Vietnamese for centuries, and the shooting and bombing was happening far from our village. We continued our peaceful life of subsistence and mutual sharing which had continued for generations despite continual threats from neighboring peoples and overbearing rulers.

One thing my people never heard on their radios, though, was any Christian broadcast. We never heard that the supreme God had revealed himself through his son, the Lord Jesus Christ. We didn't know we had a savior.

The people of my village were religious, however. Early every morning, the yellow-robed Buddhist monks and their novices walked through the village to receive the food offerings, with their bowls hanging from their necks. They stood at each corner ringing their bells, waiting for people from each house to bring them the daily rice and other foods.

My mother gave me the responsibility of cooking the rice and taking our food offering to the monks every morning before school.

We had to remove our shoes when we approached the monks, because they were considered holy. We were not allowed to look them in the face or touch their clothing or utensils.

Each family must give a spoonful of rice to each of the monks. It must be taken from the very top of the pot of rice and dropped carefully into the Buddhists' copper bowls. If we banged the spoon on the edge of a Buddhist's bowl, it was a sin for which we would be punished in the next life.

After giving offerings of rice and other food, each little group of neighbors waited for the Buddists to bless them, then they dutifully chanted the Buddhist worship. The chants are writtcn in a language related to the Sanskrit and Pali languages. The people didn't understand the words, but the priests would teach them the meanings.

The chants were a long list of "Don'ts" or commandments. Do not kill .. Do not steal .. Do not commit adultery .. on and on. In the folk Buddhism of my people, they tried to live moral lives and accumulate enough goodness (or merit) so when they died, Buddha would take them to Heaven. If they were not good enough, they believed they would have to go to Hell for a certain number of years for each sin, then they would be reincarnated as another person or as an animal. If their sin was killing someone's ox, they would be reincarnated as an ox for punishment. Even from Heaven, one could choose to be reincarnated.

My people didn't know much about hope. But when I prayed in my heart, asking for blessings, I believed there was a supreme God who heard me.

The spirits of the dead were believed to visit the living. The people believed in angels and they feared evil spirits.

Near the temple grew a Hindu Tree of Wisdom, which was a bodhi tree, a type of fruit-bearing fig tree. In the Khmer language, we called it *Derm-po*. Asian people plant these trees next to temples in memory of the tree under which the Buddha was sitting (five centuries before Christ) when he received his "enlightenment".

Tradition says that for six years the Buddha left his life of luxury and sought to find truth and a way out of human suffering--sickness, hunger, and death--by Hindu asceticism, through extreme self-denial and self-inflicted torture. He nearly starved himself to death, but this did not bring enlightenment. In the seventh year of his search, as he meditated under the bodhi tree, he heard a wedding festival taking place. A girl was playing her stringed instrument. The sound was harsh and out of tune for the strings were all wound either too tightly or too loosely.

"Daughter," the girl's father told her, "you will make beautiful music if you don't wind the strings too tight or too loose. Find the middle where the string is perfectly in tune."

The Buddha taught that wisdom was found in a life of moderation, which he called "the middle way", not in cither extreme of self-denial or self-indulgence. One must detach himself from both the pleasures and the cares of this world in order to experience peace from corrupting desires and release from suffering. Much of the Buddha's teaching was good: seek wisdom, live a moral and ethical life, do good to others, show compassion, help the poor ... But he lived long before Christ and he never knew the light of the Gospel.

We were taught that the Buddha said a greater One than he was coming. And he forbade his followers from worshiping him or making images of him. But after his death his followers sold relics of his bones and images of the Buddha proliferated throughout Asia. Many centuries later, my people inherited the Buddhist teachings mixed with idol and relic worship, Hindu gods, spirits of nature, appeasing of demons, and ancestor worship.

People of the village would sometimes tie yellow ribbons, which they considered holy, on the Wisdom Tree, pray to it, give food to it. And in this tree people saw demons.

At times demons would become angered and would possess people and wouldn't leave them until they were appeased. The demons required people to make sacrifices of chickens, pig heads, and incense.

After my father died, my mother wanted to know what happened to his spirit. She visited the local medium or spiritist. He was an old man, the grandfather of one of my friends. His name was Ta Thong. He came from the north of Thailand. He found a wife in our village, and stayed there.

I was told that when this old man was young, he wanted to receive the power to communicate with the dead. So he did what the devil required. He killed his young common-law wife and took her three-month unborn baby, cooked and preserved it, and sacrificed it to demons.

I was scared of that old man. Children were ordinarily not allowed to go into his presence. But my mother took me and my little sister because we were the youngest children and our father loved us especially. She thought his spirit might ask, "Where are my son and my daughter?"

I hid behind my mother inside the dim, candle-lit room where the old man sat, and I peered round at him. My mother gave him money and he began calling forth the spirit of my father. He began to tremble and his eyes looked strange. I felt a wind blow and saw the candle flicker out. The old man's voice changed.

"It's really hot here," the spirit said. "Why did you call me? Who are you?"

My mother answered, thinking it was my father's spirit. Then the evil, deceiving spirit, spoke through the old man, telling my mother what she must do to have her husband released from the terrible hot place. It told her to redeem him by paying for a festival with food for the

influence on us. One day, my friend Khamphong and I hurried through our after-school chores. I fed the chickens and pigs. I cooked the rice over the fire of the outdoor kitchen. I took the water jars to the river to fill them. The rest of my family were out at the farm, working. My friend and I took a rifle shell from a bullet that had been shot in the war, and we used our imaginations and made a gun that worked.

Two papaya trees grew near our house. One tree had large fruit, plenty for us to eat. The other tree produced tiny fruit that hung down on string-like stems. That fruit wouldn't be missed, we thought. So we practiced with our homemade gun by shooting the papayas off the tree.

But my number three brother, Art, who was twenty, came home early and caught us.

In our culture the older siblings had the authority to spank and discipline the younger ones. He saw what we did and he chased us out of the yard, but we were too fast for him, and we got away.

"My brother will kill us," I said. Scared, we ran out of the village on the gravel road the government had built. We met my family on the road bringing home the cow and ox and carrying vegetables from the farm.

"Tum-Tum," my mom said, "come home now with us. Help me carry this eggplant and these long green beans."

"I can't. Art is going to kill me," I told her.

"We'll protect you," said my number four brother, Nonglam.

Khamphong and I followed them to my house, but when we saw Art, we took the cow under the house to tether it, and we hid behind one of the smooth, carved wooden pillars that held up the house.

But my brother saw us. He was making a charcoal fire in the kitchen stove for cooking.

"I'll kill you," he said.

"Yes, kill them!" called my mom, who was listening from inside the living room of the house. By now, she had heard what we had done.

We thought they meant it. We ran away on the road again, deciding to go to Kampong's farm. But it was dark and scary and we had heard about the "headless man" who was out there, the ghost of a man who was killed about twenty years earlier during an uprising against the French. In the dark, we ran home and sneaked back under the house. We could hear the family above us in the house talking.

"Those kids are bad to play with guns. I want to teach them a lesson," Art said and my mom and Kampong's mother agreed.

Too scared to go up to the house, we climbed into the tamarind tree. We had missed supper and felt hungry. As we ate sour tamarind leaves, we looked out across the darkness at the sugar palm tree in the neighbor's yard. Then we remembered that a dead man had just been cremated under that tree, and some of his ashes and bones were buried there.

We believed that dead people's spirits lingered for seven days, before they realized they were dead and went to another place. The neighbor had died only a few days earlier. As was the custom with my people, we had honored the dead man with rituals and celebrations lasting three days. Relatives and friends had gathered to wash, dress, and prepare the man's body, laying him in a praying position with a candle and incense in his hands. Other candles and incense were burned, the people feasted, the monks chanted, and relatives prayed to the angel of death to take the dead man's spirit across the river of death. The third day, the man's body was cremated in the back yard. Some of his bones were collected in a jar and set in the mausoleum at the temple, where relatives would light candles in his honor to help him in his next life.

As we hid in the tamarind tree, surrounded by spooky-looking branches and palm leaves we thought: *What if the ghost comes to haunt us in the night?* Suddenly the silence was broken by the sound of a heavy fruit falling from the sugar palm tree near the grave. It frightened the rats who lived under the leaves that littered the ground. The rats skampered and ran, making a sound that we thought could be the dead man's spirit. We knew spirits liked to go up trees. We scurried down from the tamarind, but Khamphong's shirt caught on a branch.

"Help, help, the ghost is grabbing me," cried Khamphong.

I said, "Don't cry out too loud. My brother will hear us."

We ran into the barn where the rice was stored. We hid behind a sack of rice and tried to sleep. But up in the doorway in the moonlight, we could see a human hand dangling there. (Actually, hand-shaped sugar palm leaves had been placed there.) We couldn't sleep.

In the morning my number four brother, Nonglam, came outside to use the outhouse. He was carrying a stick used for spanking the cows. Just in case we were in the barn, when he walked by, he whacked the barn with his stick.

"Come out!" he said.

I kept quiet.

"I surrender," Khamphong cried and walked out.

My mom was surprised to find I had spent the night out there. When she realized what a fright we had and how seriously we had taken their teasing, she was sorry. I learned not to get carried away teasing children. Because they will believe you.

As a child I dreamed of doing something good with my life and becoming someone important if opportunity was given. I didn't know that someday God would give me salvation and the opportunity to serve in His Kingdom.

I believe every child has the ambition of growing up to be like their role model. That is why we should give God's words to the children when He sends them to us.

Life of the Water Lily

If you tell me the story
I will paint the picture in my mind.
If you speak, I will hear the words.

I am the water lily's seed
buried in the soil of the dry pond,
waiting to receive rain in its season.

When water fills the pond,
I will burst through the muddy soil.
I will grow strong above the water.

God gives sunlight and rain.
So I will give flowers,
and pollen to the bees,
and before the dry season,
seeds to the next generation.

-- Physa Chanmany

41

Map #2

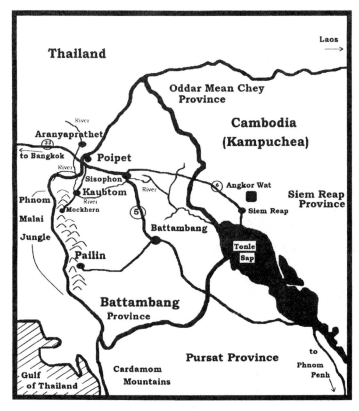

Battambang Province in northwest Cambodia, during Physa's childhood, before 1975.

Pictured in map:

Thailand -- Country through which Physa's ancestors migrated from Laos. Thailand controlled Battambang and Siem Reap provinces in the early part of the twentieth century, influencing its culture and language.

Angkor Wat -- World-famous ruins. Center of Medieval Khmer Kingdom.

Phnom Malai -- Tropical rain forest along Thai border, rich in wildlife, near which Physa's Lao-Khmer tribe settled, cleared rice farms, and established a village.

Kaubtom -- Physa's childhood village. His grandfather remembered when elephants walked through the village, before the government built the gravel road through Kaubtom for hauling logs from the jungle for export. When Physa and his friends first saw the logging trucks and tractors drive by, they started modeling little replicas with their earth clay.

Monkhern -- The last village before the border, deep in the jungle. Physa remembers wandering into this village as a boy while grazing the cattle. The people chased him away, saying, "Don't let your cows eat my garden!" With the jungle too dense for growing rice, they lived by growing small vegetables gardens and harvesting tropical fruits, bamboo, and wood to trade in the city for rice.

Pailin -- The hilly area near this town produces rubies and other gem stones.

Poipet -- The closest town to Kaubtom, but the villagers seldom went there to trade, because underpaid government workers at border patrols would stop them and charge exhorbitant "taxes" for goods they carried to or from market.

Sisophon -- The town where the Kaubtom villagers did their trading and got newspapers.

Tonle Sap -- The great lake which is one of the richest sources of fresh water fish in the world. In rainy season, it swells and flows back into many rivers, which flood, watering and enriching rice paddies and carrying fish across the land.

3. Harvest and Courtship

Before plowing and planting in May, the farmers sacrificed chickens, burned incense, and gave fragrant flowers to the spirits that inhabited the fields. They prayed to the spirits to protect their growing crops, bless them with rain fall, and keep insects away. In return, they promised to honor the spirits at harvest time.

In June the heavy rains fell, lakes and rivers swelled, and farmers waded into the flooded rice paddies to transplant rice seedlings into the muddy soil.

While the rice crops grew, we raised squash, long green beans, sweet potatoes, tata root, corn, eggplant, red potatoes, peppers, and soy beans in raised beds that were actually huge termite nests left there when the farmers cleared the rice fields of jungle growth. These mounds kept the vegetable plants out of the flooded fields and provided rich soil for our gardens.

In their generation, my grandparents worked the farm with water buffalo. My parents used oxen. My mother kept several steers, cows, and calves. The cattle became pets to us, and they provided extra income when we sold newborn calves.

During the school break, November through January, we children spent days and nights out at our family farms, sleeping in grass huts built on wooden platforms.

Waking before sunrise, I looked out at the surrounding jungle trees and I thought I saw monsters and ghosts. But the sunlight revealed forest and fields teeming with color and life: tropical trees budded fresh, green growth; brown leaves fell and littered the ground; armies of ants and termites built huge nests, some on trees, some in the ground; butterflies, caterpillars, and birds of all sizes and colors flitted and fluttered in the canopy.

We quickly cooked and ate breakfast, for there was work to do and each family member had a responsibility. My job was to chase away the hordes of little birds that swooped down on the rice fields morning and evening, hiding low in the grass to eat the maturing grains. Through the paddy I walked banging tin cans. Hundreds of birds flapped out of the grasses, buzzing like helicopters, back to the jungle trees where they sang all the hot, rainy day.

The green-, yellow-, and red-headed parrots were smarter. They dashed down from the trees, pecked off the heads of rice, then sped back to safety in the high branches. My older brothers outsmarted the parrot birds, though. Fashioning wooden propellers of hard, fresh wood and attaching tails of long, dry grasses to catch the wind, they set these contraptions atop bamboo poles. When the propellers whirred like airplanes in the wind, the pesky birds stayed away.

Ever present were groups of white herons, black herons, and cranes wading in the wet fields, but the big birds didn't eat rice. They searched for snails, small shrimps, and fishes. Cattle egrets rode on the backs of the buffalo and oxen as they grazed on the grass, pecking ticks and blood-sucking flies off the animals. Black birds often joined them.

When the wind blew my way, the sweet scent of pumpkins and of white, green, and golden melons ripening in my mom's garden mounds gave me a big appetite. For lunch, we ate a meal of rice, pork, and fish.

During the day, we children watched the oxen and cows. At nine or ten, I was still too small to see over the tall grasses. And little calves would get lost in the grass, also; then we had to search for them in the evening. So we children climbed up into the trees to watch the cattle from above. And we kept our ears attuned to always listen for the lead cow's bell.

In the evening, as we small children prepared to sleep, our big brothers gave us instructions.

"You guys make sure you look around and see where the pigeon doves roost, so we can shoot them."

As the sun set, we watched big flocks of birds--up to a hundred at a time--whoosh up from the ground, encircle a tree, and settle to roost on its branches, blackening the tree. After dark, our big brothers took their flash lights and sling shots and a scarf for carrying the birds. They'd bring back four or five of those pigeons to cook the next day.

Later, when the wolves howled eerily, we small children quit talking and scooted closer to our big brothers to feel safe and fall asleep. In the morning, we'd see fresh wolf tracks nearby in the damp soil, where the wolves came to eat the fishes that receding waters had left in the ponds.

At the end of the harvest, when we carried our rice and vegetables to the village on ox carts late evenings, we often caught sight of wolves. At night, then, I was glad to be snug in my bed, back in our village home. The soft cotton-stuffed mattresses and pillows felt good.

Cotton was a leading crop of our country. In my grandmother's and mother's generations, they milled the cotton and wove the fabric by hand to make clothing, scarves, and blankets. But in our generation, people bought fabric and clothing in the city, made of factory-milled cotton.

We had a type of cotton (kapok) that grew on trees which we called *derm-go* (silk-cotton trees). Each family planted one or two of these large trees in their rambling, verdant yards. The thick, long branches reached high in the canopy. The tree produced white blossoms in late December, and their sweet scent filled the evening air. Under a full moon, we could see the fruit bats fly up into the silk-cotton trees and drink the sweet nectar from the flowers.

Our silk-cotton trees produced six-inch fruit that could be eaten. But when we let the fruit dry on the trees, the fibers inside turned to a light, fluffy, cottony substance. Left unpicked, the hard shells of the fruit cracked in the summer sun and fluff flew on the wind, covering houses and yards. If people were lazy, they left it. But my mom and grandma were industrious.

"The cotton is ready. Go get it for us," they told us children.

We gathered the cotton fruit and our mom and grandma stuffed pillows and mattresses for the whole family. One or two trees kept us supplied with fresh bedding.

We children picked extra cotton fruit and traded them for rubber bands from people in the village who had gone to the city. (Our country had many rubber plantations.) We played games with the rubber bands, or used them to trade with our friends for other things, such as marbles.

In late January, the rains stopped, the water drained from the paddies, the grass died, and the rice ripened in the sun. The farmers cut off the heads of rice. The whole village freely grazed their cattle on the stalks that were left and they also saved straw for feeding the cattle during festival days when no one wanted to take them out to graze.

After January, with all the rice in the barn, the fields were burned, and it was time to celebrate and give thanks for the harvest. The Buddhist monks organized the harvest festival, dividing the village into sections. In each section of fifteen or twenty homes, the monks built a tent, which the people decorated with green palm leaves and flowers and pictures and images of the Buddha. On the floor mat, villagers placed their food offerings.

The monks took a large ball of cotton string, tied it inside the tent, then unwound it from home to home, connecting every house and barn in the neighborhood. All the people held on to the string as the monks inside the tent chanted thanks for the crops and blessings for the people, believing the Buddhist blessing ran from the tent through the cotton string to each barn and home.

People joyfully thanked the gods; they thanked the spirits of the farm; and they thanked the good angels, which they believed came from a higher god, though they didn't know the name of that God.

In the evening everyone drank sweetened condensed milk and tea.

On festival nights, the monks ran a generator to light the village so we could celebrate in the cool of the night. Sometimes they rented a movie from the city and projected it onto a large white cloth stretched between trees in someone's backyard.

The older youth, like my big brothers, liked meeting friends during the festivals. Boys and girls talked together in groups, enjoying an opportunity to get acquainted.

After the hard work of harvest, courtship season began. Groups of boys and girls chatted as they took the herds of cattle out to the farms to graze the rice stalks. We young children sometimes followed them and listened in on the conversations. Later, I teased my big brother, repeating the words I heard him say to a girl.

"You are the parrot bird. You are the lilly flower." I laughed and my brother chased me.

In the evenings the big boys would dress in their best clothes (loose, pajama-like trousers and brightly colored, flower-print shirts) and promenade along the village paths in the moonlight. They carried flashlights on dark nights.

I would lie in bed in the late evening, hearing groups of older boys walk by--talking, singing, and playing bamboo instruments or mandolin-like stringed instruments. Then I thought to myself, *I want to grow up and promenade and sing like that.*

Groups of older girls waited on the verandahs of their houses, dressed in colorful sarongs and blouses, weaving grass mats in the light of homemade kerosene lamps. They had gathered the grasses earlier that day. Boys and girls (always in groups) talked in the lamplight, while the girls worked, and the parents listened and watched from inside the house. The father might be smoking a cigar or weaving cattle ropes of bark. The mom would be working in the house, and putting the small children to bed, while the young people were courting.

My two rebellious brothers, Boun and Art, often stayed out too late, and my mom lectured them. (Soon and Nonglam were good boys, strong farmers, and helped our mom.)

51

My number two brother, Soon, married in 1970, when he was twenty and I was about ten. God blessed us that year--though we didn't know him yet--with a rice crop so large, it didn't fit in our barn. We stored extra bags of rice under the house. Then, we were ready when Soon announced his love for a girl, and the girl's parents, agreeing to the marriage, told my mom what they required for a dowry. My mom, a widow, was able to afford it, because of our huge harvest that year.

The school teachers taught us the legend of the dowry. Long ago, many customs of our people came from India, where the dowry is still paid by the bride's family. When the great Khmer Kingdom ruled much of Southeast Asia, and the magnificent Hindu temple at Angkor Wat was built, the prince and the princess made an agreement. The prince and all the young men would build one part of the temple; and the princess and all the girls would build another part of the temple. The last group to finish their section would have to pay the dowry from then on.

But the women tricked the men. Since the work was done at night, the princess said to the prince, "Each morning when the morning star reaches to the top branches of the sugar palm tree, everyone must stop working." The prince and the men agreed.

So every night all the people worked. And each morning before daylight, the girls took an artificial star they made and put it high in the sugar palm tree and lighted it with a candle. The men saw the "star" and stopped working, but the girls kept working until sunrise. This continued for years; and the girls finished first. Their trick worked, and ever since then, the groom's family has paid the dowry. (This story is typical of how my people were selective in the customs they took from India.)

Generally, men married between the ages of twenty and twenty-five, and girls between the ages of sixteen and twenty. An unmarried man of thirty or an unmarried lady of twenty-five were considered too old to be marriageable, and the mother had to search hard to find that son or daughter a mate.

The wedding feast lasted three days, providing an opportunity for relatives and friends to gather and young people to socialize.

53

The first day of the wedding, the young men cut fire wood, counted the pigs and chickens and dug the pits for roasting them. The ladies prepared sticky rice balls stuffed with bananas, sticky rice cakes, palm sugar pastry rolled in grated coconut, and jackfruit pudding. My mother was known for her rice wine, and she made this for my brother's wedding. Everyone gathered on the verandah of the house, talking, laughing, and joking together as they worked.

The second day, the groom's family and friends assembled under the banana palms and mango trees, dressed in their nicest clothes, carrying all the items of the dowry that the bride's family had required: platters of fruit; baskets of desserts and other foods; gifts of clothing, perfume, and gold jewelry; ornate silver jars filled with money. All the people, escorting the groom, filed in a long procession down the village paths, all the way to the bride's family home. The people sang and danced and carried the dowry, gifts, and flowers for the bride's family.

Before they reached her house, the bride and her attendants and parents came walking out in their own procession to receive the groom and his dowry. The bride wore a traditional dress of hand-woven, soft red silk, bracelets and anklets, with her hair pinned up in curls and adorned with flowers. The groom wore a long linen shirt and silk trousers that are traditional to both Khmer and Lao people. They came face to face, the bride lowered her eyes and pressed her palms together to show respect, and right there, an elderly person spoke to the bride about how to respect her husband, how to speak to him, and other rules of marriage.

At the bride's home, everyone took off their shoes before entering the house, and the bride washed the feet of the groom and of the elderly guests (either that, or she paid a young child to wash the feet).

The elders, dressed in white shirts, performed the wedding ceremony, lecturing the bride and groom about loyalty to their parents, faithfulness to each other, and following the traditions of the elders. Then came the ritual chants in the Pali language of the Theravada Buddhist scriptures. The orchestra played ancient Khmer instruments, singers sang and dancers danced, moving slowly and gently in a circle, gesturing gracefully with their hands.

Incense burned, the Buddha's image was displayed prominently, a pig head was offered to the spirits of the ancestors, and the elders called on the spirits of nature, the angels, and the ancestors to come and bless the couple.

The third day of the wedding, the guests feasted and celebrated with more singing, dancing, and talking and laughing together. The guests gave money instead of gifts to the couple. Again, the elders stood before the bride and groom and taught them the laws for the wife to submit to her husband, and the husband to submit to the bride's parents, and both of them to submit to the elders. They must now live in a different way, with responsibility for each other and for their home. A singer crooned words such as these:

You are like the moon and the flower.
I pledge to you my love forever...

Then everyone returned home, including the groom. Later that night, the best man took the groom to the bride's house, and there he stayed. The couple lived with the bride's family for six months to two years, until the new husband proved his ability to work and support his wife.

"Okay, you can go and start your own home now," the father-in-law would say.

The parents would either give land to the couple or help them buy it, build a house, and cultivate a farm.

Besides celebrating festivals and marriages, during the dry season men of the village hunted in the forest for meat or cut down trees and sawed wood. They sold some of the good, hard wood in the city. And the rest they stored in the village for building houses as marriages were anticipated, the rainy seasons came again and again, and the rice crops continued to be harvested.

4. The First Exodus

As war raged in the eastern part of the country, we heard shooting in the distance; but it never came close enough to affect our village directly. The national army was busy fighting a civil war with the Khmer Communists, called the *Khmer Rouge,* whom the Chinese were aiding toward their goal of winning control of the country. This distracted our peace-keeping national army from their usual job of guarding the Thai border, which was a dense, wild jungle through which thieves could reach our village.

On the spring festival day of 1975, all the villagers were gone from their homes. The people--young and old--gathered for several days and nights in the Buddhist center for worship, music, and food. Food concessions offered such delicacies as roast chicken, beef on a stick, sugar cane sticks, cookies, and candies. Children liked the lollipops. Adults drank rice wine and smoked. The old people were still old fashioned; they came for the Buddhist rituals, to chant, burn incense, and to get something from their gods or accumulate merit for their next life or for their dead relatives. The kids went for fun. The youth went to chat with their friends, listen to music, and watch Thai movies on a big screen set up outdoors.

The ladies wore their lovely silk sarongs (instead of the usual cotton ones), and the men wore their best, colorful clothing.

My mother sat in the corner with the older folk. They listened to old-fashioned Asian music and drama called *Mo-Laam*. We young people had become impatient with the long love ballads that told discreet, subtle stories and used flowery, poetic imagery.

"To me you are the flower, the bee, the sunshine, the rain," the singers crooned. Other songs described the singer's feelings about his farm or his land.

Up until the 1960's, the village people still performed these traditional songs for each other. By the early 1970's, the people had prospered from their large rice crops, and they hired professional musicians from Thailand to perform at the village festivals: three or four singers, and two men playing bamboo mouth instruments.

My generation found the old ways and music boring. We hired our own music, bands that came from the city to play the more direct and daring music of the sixties and seventies, including western songs by the Beatles.

During these later festivals, the Buddhist monks found profane ways to raise money. My people were beginning to compromise their traditional moral values and high ethical standards.

That fateful year, while the entire village was preoccupied at the festival, Thai thieves crept into our village and stole many oxen and cattle.

Then on April 17, 1975, the Khmer Rouge Communists, commanded by their leader Pol Pot, won the civil war and took over the government. They closed the borders, and they declared "peace". I remember the day those first communist soldiers marched into our village.

They wore black, Chinese-made uniforms and long scarves. Some were very young, only thirteen or fourteen years of age. They had not had enough to eat, and were very skinny, with ghost-like faces. They did not look friendly. But they spoke very politely, always addressing people as "younger brother", "older brother", "aunt", or "uncle".

"Grandmother, may we have a mango from your tree?" they'd ask. Or, "Brother, may we stay under your house?"

This way, they deceptively won the hearts of the village people. They used the name of the Kampuchean royal prince, said they were working for him, and told everyone to give them their guns, other weapons, and valuables.

"We are starting a program of re-education," the officers announced. "We have a new system now. The old roots and the old system must be destroyed."

They said we must leave our homes, farms, temple, school, and river.

"We have to train you in the new ways. Let's go."

So they chased all the villagers out of their houses and took us away from our village about 20 kilometers into the jungle, to a meadow area along a creek, closer to Thailand. On both banks of the creek, in a long single row on each side, we built little huts with grass roofs--nothing like the homes to which we were accustomed. All of my aunts' and uncles' huts were built on the east side, about one kilometer away from our hut. All the huts were quite spread out, which made communicating with each other difficult.

We had to clear fields and plant crops with the "new" (primitive) methods of farming. This place was called *Ohpophool*, or Wild Creek.

Many fish lived in the creek, and rabbits nearby. My mom didn't realize the danger we were in, and she told me to go back to our village and get some fishing hooks.

I walked the 20 kilometers through jungle area and across our farms. I first came to a home where lived a woman who was a family friend. She greeted me and took me into her house and fed me. She explained to me that I should not be out on my own, that the Khmer Rouge would shoot anyone they found going back to the village. She was allowed to stay and live in her own house because she was a relative of one of the Khmer Rouge officers. She took me to him. Because of her, he wrote a letter and gave it to me.

"Wherever you go, take this letter with you for protection and show it to anyone who stops you. In this country, you no longer travel freely on your own," he warned. The God whose name I didn't yet know was protecting me.

They allowed me to go to my house to get the fishing hooks. I was shocked to find strangers living in our home.

They said, "We are the *old people,* before-the-18th-of-April people, who have belonged to the party a long time. Angka wants us to live in the houses. You are *new people*, since we liberated you on the 18th of April. Now, everything belongs to Angka, the party. This is not your house anymore."

The Khmer Rouge assigned five soldiers at a time to stay in our make-shift village and guard us and supervise our work. For two months we lived under surveillance that way. I was fourteen years old.

My friends and I didn't mind the change at first. We climbed to the treetops to watch the cattle. While up in the trees, we played games. One day we boys played our game of "monkey". One guy was on the ground--he was "it"--he was the man trying to catch the monkeys. The rest of us were monkeys trying to keep away from the man. We jumped from tree to tree and swung from branch to branch. I caught hold of a branch and it broke and I landed on the ground. My arm was broken. The bone stuck out through my skin.

Scientific medicine was outlawed by the Khmer Rouge (as were all things western). A medicine man said he knew how to fix my arm. He made a bamboo "cast" for my arm and tied it with a scarf for a sling. The bone did not heal straight.

Soon after I broke my arm, everything changed. I couldn't run and play with the other children. Instead, I listened to the adults talking. Many of the villagers saw hard times coming in Kampuchea. As their ancestors had done before them, they wanted to flee from their oppressors, rather than become their slaves.

At this time, fifteen Thai men sneaked back into our camp carrying guns from the war; and I don't know why my village people trusted those men, but the Thai offered to help my people escape. Every family secretly started packing their things.

"Tum, you are naughty," my mom teased me. "You broke your arm. Now you can't run. When we go, we will leave you behind."

"I can still run fast, even though it hurts," I told her.

The day came. Whispers spread from hut to hut. "When you hear shooting, run ..."

Before sundown, the Khmer Rouge guards had laid aside their guns and were cooking their dinner outdoors. The Thai took several villagers, whose faces were known and trusted, to the guards. They hid their guns under their clothes and acted friendly. The village men had come from the farm and were carrying large machetes used to clear the fields.

"Brothers, can we have some smokes?" they asked as they approached the guards in a friendly manner.

The men all smoked together and drank tea. Suddenly the villagers rose up and took the guards by surprise, hacking with their knives, killing them all. Then for fear of reprisal from the Khmer Rouge base of soldiers nearby, the Thai shot their guns over and over into the air. The soldiers heard the shots and thought it sounded like a large army, so they hesitated before coming.

When the people heard the shooting, they panicked, and began to grab their packs and run toward the forest of trees for cover and to find the escape route northwest into Thailand. I saw people all around me running and yelling. I heard my brother and sister say, "Run, Tum."

I ran. I thought my family was coming behind me. And I wanted to prove to them that I could still run fast and keep up, even though my broken arm hurt.

I heard my mom's voice calling out, "Tum, come back. Wait for your brother."

I kept going, thinking my family would all follow. I ran with the people into the jungle. Darkness fell. I could no longer hear my mom calling.

I stopped. My siblings were not coming behind me. All the people ran on and I found myself alone. Should I go on and catch up and join my friends and relatives heading toward the Thai border, and wait for my mother and brothers and sisters to come after me? I hesitated in the dark forest.

Should I go back? I was afraid I would go back and my mom wouldn't be there. But all the others left me; could I find them up ahead in the thick darkness? I was afraid of getting lost in the jungle.

In the darkness, if you stepped on a wasp nest, their stings could kill. The sharp grasses could cut your skin, and in the grass, snakes were hiding. People had their eyes poked out by twigs hanging from low growing trees. And then there were the wolves that we heard howling during the rainy season.

I risked going back. My waiting mother explained that she didn't want the family to be separated. My family had planned to leave, but then when the time came, my older, married brother Soon could not go. His wife and daughter had become sick with the flu and couldn't run. Besides that, Soon's elderly father-in-law had hurt his leg and had to walk with a cane.

Many of my aunts and uncles on both my mother's and father's sides of the family had lived in our village; and we didn't know if they had all escaped or not.

Thirty Khmer Rouge soldiers, who heard the shooting, entered our camp that night. But they didn't pursue the escapees, for two reasons: first, it had started to rain hard; second, they heard so much gunfire that they feared a huge group of armed Thai.

The Khmer Rouge searched the village and found that everyone had their things packed as if ready to leave also. They questioned my mother.

"You tried to escape, too. See, you have packed your things."

"No, I have my things packed because this is not my home," she told them. "I was chased out of my home and made to come here, and I don't have a place for everything yet."

The Khmer Rouge Communists didn't believe our stories.

"Count off how many are left," an officer ordered the soldiers. "We have to put them to sleep." I got in line, but I didn't understand what was happening. Why were the elderly people crying? I asked my mom.

"We're going to die, Tum. If you get a chance to run, then run."

The Communist soldiers made us form a line and count off. We looked down the line. That is when we found out that all our aunts and uncles on both sides of our family had escaped. Of all our relatives, my family alone were left.

The soldiers prepared to shoot us.

I felt numb. I felt like I had no blood in my body.

"An angel will help us," my mom told me.

Frightened and angry, I responded, "Why didn't you let me go? Why didn't we leave my brother? There is no angel, no god to help us now."

But later I would come to know the truth and to realize that even as we faced death, God was there helping us.

For at that moment, as we waited to be shot, another officer--a wise and courageous man, unusual in Pol Pot's army--spoke up.

"No, we shouldn't shoot them," he said. "Just take them away. If some of your fingers are frozen, you don't cut off all your good fingers and your whole hand. Only cut off the fingers that are frozen."

"Don't worry," he told us. He was an intelligent and handsome man.

"We aren't going to kill you. You didn't escape. You stayed here."

Two men were not so fortunate. A man from the nearby village of Viengmuang wanted to escape with the others, but he arrived a day late. He was carrying a pack.

"I just came to visit," he told the Khmer Rouge. But they didn't believe him. They shot and killed him. His name was Ta-Jon.

Then the soldiers found an eighty year-old man named Yee who was left lying in the jungle, unable to keep up with the exodus. The Khmer Rouge shot him.

They forced my brother to bury the dead.

The killing had started.

Many of the villagers escaped that night. They made a good choice. Years later I learned what happened to them. After they fled ten or fifteen kilometers into the jungle, the Thai men told the villagers to sit down in a field.

"We wanted to make sure you were safe first," the Thai said. "Now we expect you to pay us 150 baht per person."

That was a large amount of Thai money for the people to pay. In desperation they took out the gold and other valuables they had hidden in their packs. Finally, the Thai were satisfied.

"Okay, follow us and we'll take you safely to the Thai border," the men said. But in the darkness, the bandits ran off and disappeared in the night. Left on their own, the villagers would easily have been found by the Khmer Rouge soldiers, if the soldiers had chosen to follow. Without question, all the people would have been killed.

God was watching over that group of villagers, many of whom were my friends and relatives. They reached the Thai border in three days. Those people later became refugees in America and many became Christians and are now worshiping the Lord Jesus Christ as members of a Lao-Cambodian church in Long Beach, California.

We still speak of that escape as "The First Exodus".

After that, the Khmer Rouge watched the rest of us very closely, putting us all in huts close together in a group. The soldiers told us not to go far into the woods, even for "going to the bathroom", or they would consider us trying to escape and shoot us.

Three days later--unbeknown to us, it was the same day that the escapees reached Thailand--the Khmer Rouge Communists soldiers guarding us announced that they were taking the remainder of us on a second exodus.

71

12th Century Angkor Wat is the largest and most famous of the Temples of Angkor, one of the architectural wonders of the world. Constructed when the Khmer Kingdom covered much of present-day Vietnam, Laos, and Thailand, this vast and intricate building project undertaken by Khmer kings to honor Hindu deities, Angkor is said to have no equal in the history of humanity. *Photo reproduced courtesy of Southeast Asian Outreach.*

Skulls from the killing fields. 17,000 men, women, children, and infants were bludgeoned to death and left lying in a mass grave after being detained and tortured in Tuol Sleng prison, in Phnom Penh between 1975 and 1978. Under the Khmer Rouge regime, over twenty-five percent of Cambodia's population was killed or allowed to die of starvation and disease. *Photo reproduced courtesy of Southeast Asian Outreach.*

5. The Killing Fields

The soldiers in our make-shift camp barked orders.

"Everyone must leave here. Take only what you need for three days. Give everything else you own to the government." My family took some rice, an ox, food, and clothes. We joined the exodus, going far to the east.

We walked one week on a highway. The soldiers watched us on the road and from trees above to be sure we didn't get off the road, even for reasons of personal sanitation. People had to climinate on the road, where they also had to sleep at night.

They took us far from our home to a hostile, dry place of barren fields with no natural sources of food and no store. Again they commanded us to build huts, though this time there were no trees. We built them out of grasses. For fuel to make fires for cooking food, we had to cut dry grass and collect cow manure.

They held us there like slaves for about six months, and we kept expecting to be allowed to return home. For one month we were okay, then we got hungry.

"All the farms belong to *Angka*, the party," the Khmer Rouge told us. They separated all the people of our country by age groups and forced us to work on collective farms and projects. Like cattle, the people were herded out of villages and cities, even out of the capital, Phnom Penh, to work for the Khmer Rouge Communist government.

The children had to dig ditches. The youth and single adults had to dig and build dams and canals. The government believed if they could manage the water resources of the country, they could force the rice crops to grow all year long. Married couples with their small children were put in villages to work where their skills were needed. Mothers were allowed to keep nursing children with them only. When a child was weaned, it was taken from its mother, because children belonged to *Angka*.

Temples, libraries, schools, museums, and hospitals were burnt; musical instruments and works of art were destroyed; books and all printed material were forbidden; everything that belonged to the old system and culture was destroyed. Currency was outlawed. All western influences were cut off. Professionals, doctors, teachers, and all educated people were sought out and killed. The physically weak were worked to death.

The Communists tried to "purify" Khmer society of all "contamination" and make everyone work, completely dependent on the "organization", which they told us was infallible. They forbade religious beliefs and practice. They destroyed Buddhist books and images. But they gave the Buddhist monks a choice.

"If you will become civilians and work on the farms, we will not kill you."

The monks discarded their yellow robes and blended into the work camps.

Everyone had to wear black uniforms or dye their clothes black by soaking them in water in which black tree bark was boiled. We wore sandals the communists made out of old tires.

In 1975 I was 15, small and skinny. They sent me to a children's camp. Many children were housed together in a "room" without walls in which poles were planted in the ground and hammocks hung between them for sleeping. At first I thought it was an adventure to get away on my own, away from family. Then after two or three weeks, I realized I couldn't go back to my family and home, even if I wanted. I couldn't see my mom when I wanted. I was hungry; and I couldn't eat when I wanted. I wasn't free.

If a child cried for loneliness or fear in the night, the guards put him or her out in the dark alone to "learn courage". We were treated like military. In the morning a bell was rung and we had to get up immediately, before daylight. Then a second bell told us to line up. An officer with a gun lectured us.

The soldiers indoctrinated the children, telling us over and over that *Angka,* the party would take care of us and lead us to wealth, just like our glorious ancestors who built the Angkor Wat using sheer willpower and the physical strength of the people. They said we had to be self-sufficient. And they tried to teach us to hate Europeans and Americans. They told us that the Western countries were all rocky and couldn't grow rice; that if we didn't sell them rice, they would die; that we would defeat them this way.

Then the children were taken out to the fields to work. From morning until late at night we had to dig dirt, fertilize crops, plant rice, and cut grass. We were each given a small bowl of watery rice daily. Only during harvest did we get any other food. We were hungry; we were starving.

We were told if we found food we must give it to the guards to distribute. The smart, sneaky ones survived by finding fish, snails, crabs, and certain green leaves that we knew how to identify. We had to quickly break the crabs open and eat them while we were working and the guards weren't looking. I saw many children die of starvation and disease.

I felt sorry to see the farm oxen over-worked and underfed also. Many of the animals died.

Occasionally a former villager came through the camp on an errand for the party.

"Have you seen my family?" we would ask.

This way I learned of my family's location and that they were alive. But my mother never came to see me. Sometimes mothers were

76

allowed to visit their children, if they were bold and conniving.

The children who did not submit to the authority of the Khmer Rouge guards were shot. If they talked at night, broke other rules, or if the communists found anything suspicious in their past, those children were shot. Some were killed in front of the other children as examples. Others were taken out quietly in the night to be shot, their bodies left to rot on the ground, and never mentioned again.

When I first saw these killings, I shook all over, my heart raced, I felt sick to my stomach. But after a while, I became numb to the killings.

"Well, sometime it will be me," I thought. "If I don't die now, it will be later."

When I turned sixteen, the communists took me to a youth camp--a two or three day walk away--and even further from my mother.

The first year at youth camp we were fed well so we could work harder building a dam for the government to conserve water. Every morning the Communists preached to us.

"There is no God," they said with empty, cold looks on their faces. "You are god. There are no angels, no spirits."

Outwardly I submitted; but inwardly, I knew they were wrong. I had seen the work of demons in my childhood village. And I saw them now, only in a different form. Demons learn very quickly to adapt to any system. In the killing fields I saw demons at work in the starvation, in the hate, and in the killing.

Week after week, the communists interrogated each youth. With the demon-like faces of the Khmer Rouge officers before us, we were asked:

"Who did you associate with before 1975? Who were your parents? Who did they associate with?"

If you were Vietnamese, they killed you. If your parents worked for the government, they killed you. If you wore glasses, you were thought to be educated, so they killed you. If your hands were soft, you must have been rich, so they killed you. If you were handicapped and could not work, they killed you.

After questioning, people were awakened in the night.

"Okay, pack your things," they told the sleepy youth. "The government wants you to go to work in a different place now. Let's go."

These people were led out of the camp and never seen again. Many of them were marched far from the camp and shot. Corpses were left lying in the open to rot and birds and wolves would eat their flesh. Sometimes the soldiers left bodies lying close enough so we would see them when we worked in the fields or when we were sent to collect firewood. Often we could smell the stink of rotting flesh. Sometimes we would try to cover the bodies with dirt.

I also saw demons at work in the fear and cowering of the people. I saw people's hands bound with thin cords that they could easily have broken; yet these people knelt in submission to be shot or beaten to death. These prisoners might be lined up and guarded by a mere boy with a stick, yet they did not resist.

In the harvest season, the Khmer Rouge allowed young adults to marry. The soldiers held marriage ceremonies in groups of ten to twenty people. They allowed no dowry, no religious ritual, no blessing by the elders. The ceremony consisted of a soldier holding up a rifle and declaring that the couples must be faithful to each other from now on, or they will be shot. For anyone caught betraying their husband or wife, there was no divorce court. The rifle was the court.

After all the hard work of the harvest by those who survived, the rice was taken away from the starving people and sent to the Chinese government along with cotton, salt, and wood to repay the Chinese Communists for the war weapons they had given the Khmer Rouge.

In 1979, at the youth work camp, we could hear big guns from the Russian-backed Vietnamese invasion. Within two weeks, the Vietnamese Communists captured Phnom Penh. The battered Khmer Rouge Communists and their leader Pol Pot began retreating deep into the mountains and jungles along the Thai border.

We watched Khmer Rouge soldiers march past on the highway near where we worked. In some cases, they forced the youth from the camps to join their army and go into hiding with them. But they didn't take anyone from our camp. They just left us as if they had forgotten us.

The Khmer Rouge had controlled us for three years, eight months, and twenty days. We could hardly believe that the reign of terror was over. Piles of human bones lay in open fields across the country. (Later it would be estimated that out of a population of eight million people in our country, 1.5 million died under the Khmer Rouge regime.) And though the Vietnamese, whom we had considered to be our enemies now appeared to be our saviors, suffering was not over for this country of *Suffering-Healing.*

After the Khmer Rouge guards had been gone from our camp for five days, we got up the courage to leave. Thank God, the Khmer Rouge did not return to our camp.

I began walking the long road to find my mom, not knowing if all my family members were alive or dead.

She was waiting for me. She gave me a big hug, which was not the usual practice. As another way to show her affection, she cooked good food for me: sweet potato, rice and dried fish.

I spoke to my mom in the Khmer language, which had become my habit, since the Khmer Rouge forbade people to speak any other language on punishment of death.

"My son, don't speak to me in that language," she said. "Use the Lao language. If I am reincarnated, I don't want to be Khmer, because this country is under an evil curse."

All my siblings had returned except my number four brother, Nonglam. The family waited a week, then he arrived from the youth camp where he had been taken. He looked emaciated. But he was alive.

We left for our home village. We met and joined others from our village along the way. We thought we were returning home.

But the Vietnamese Communists who took over the government decided our village lay too close to the Thai border and to the jungle where the Khmer Rouge were hiding and continuing to wage guerrilla warfare. So they told us that our village would be made a ghost town. We were relocated and we were allowed to choose land to farm.

"You have two sons at home old enough to be soldiers," the Vietnamese Communist officers told my mom. "One of them must leave you to join our army."

I told my mom I would go. I knew my older and stronger brother, Nonglam, could take better care of our mother, since he was a good farmer who had worked our family farm. I had been a school boy, and I would not be as great a loss for her.

So I became a soldier at age 18. The communists trained me for a month how to shoot, crawl and dig. They gave me an M16 nearly as big as I was.

I was a soldier in the army of Heng Samrin. He was the Kampuchean president who joined with the Vietnamese Communists. I was given good food. I was allowed to go visit my mom once a month.

The Vietnamese Communists (whom we call "the second Communists") were humane compared to the Khmer Rouge Communists. Being in the army, though, was risky business, with the Khmer Rouge hiding nearby. Other bands of freedom fighters, including the Kampuchean prince and his followers, also maintained strongholds along the Thai border. Any of these guerrilla forces might attack each other at any time. And they placed land mines in the jungle, each thinking they would remember where they placed mines and avoid them. But men were even killed and maimed by their own mines.

Five of my friends (who came from my village and were also drafted into the army) and I were sent together to patrol this explosive border.

"Shoot anyone suspicious-looking," we were ordered. But we never shot anyone.

One day we spotted a man sneaking through the border, and we captured him. We recognized him as a villager we had known as children who had escaped early to Thailand. He was smuggling in medicine to exchange for gold. The Vietnamese allowed markets, so people came across the border to trade. My people purchased needed items with jewelry and other valuables they had buried in hiding places when the first Communists came.

When this man realized we had been children in his old village, he drew us a map and told us the way to escape through the jungle to Thailand, how to avoid the land mines. He gave us some medicine and we let him go.

6. Escape and New Identity

I had to decide. For me to be a communist soldier could mean having to kill or be killed. Trying to escape through the jungle could well mean being killed or maimed by land mines. Crossing the border could mean being killed by Thai villagers.

But what future could I have in Kampuchea? I didn't know that my brother Boun who had run away to Laos country so long ago had joined the Vietnamese Communist army. I didn't know that Boun had been sent to Russia to learn military tactics, that he was now living in Phnom Penh, as an officer in the new regime.

If I had known, my brother could have got me out of the guerrilla jungle and taken me to the city. But my life would have gone a different direction. The God I was soon to meet had a plan for me.

All I knew was that death and suffering had overshadowed our lives like the canopy of this teeming, death-infested jungle. There was no way around it. I would have to try to go through it.

Since 1975, very few refugees had safely escaped from our country. The Thai villagers in the jungle along the border hated the Khmer Rouge and when they saw Khmer people crossing the border, they didn't try to find out whether they were Khmer Rouge Communists or not. They just raped and killed them.

But possible freedom waited for me on the other side, if I could get through. My friends and I decided to try escaping to Thailand.

It was August of 1979 during the rainy season, when jungle sources of food were still in short supply. Fruit on the trees were not yet ripe. We had only enough rice for a couple of days, and we could only find leaves to eat.

We boys, who had known each other in the village, trusted each other. We decided to divide in two groups, so if someone stepped on a land mine or was caught, we wouldn't all be killed. I never again heard from the boys in the other group. My group followed the sun, going northwest through the jungle. Near the border, we dropped our guns and took off the soldier uniforms.

86

We found refugee camps just across the border. But they were self-contained, self-governed, not protected by the Thai government. These camps had become bases for the warring factions.

The first camp we came to was called *Nong Chann.* No shelters had been built yet. Refugees slept under trees, surrounded by flies, mosquitoes, and mud. There was not a clean water source, and no food, unless you had money or other valuables to buy food from the Thai villagers who came during the day to try to profit from the refugees. I couldn't stay there. But I couldn't go back home, either.

I wandered around by myself, alone and hungry for two days. A man my age named Sai, who had escaped from my village to Thailand in 1975, came often to the border to see if his relatives had escaped to that camp. But he found me, instead. He gave me some food and some Thai money, the equivalent of five dollars. He had prospered in Thailand. He was wearing nice, western-style clothes.

He offered to take me to the Aranya Prathet refugee camp, where people from our old village lived. They were refugees from 1975,

87

waiting for sponsorship to the west. He said he could get me there, even though it was against the law. He knew the system.

"I will die no matter what I do; so I might as well die trying," I thought.

We left early in the morning and he paid someone to take us as far as the first border patrol. Then we were dropped off so we could sneak around the border station on foot, through the jungle and back to the road on the other side. We hitched another ride and he paid for the driver to take us as far as the next border check point. We got out again and sneaked around the border check point through the jungle and then back to the road. My friend said if we were caught, I would have to say that I was on my own, that I didn't know him.

At sunset we reached the outside of the camp. It was surrounded by forest and situated far from the nearest Thai village.

I had no I.D. and I would have to sneak into the camp.

"Tum, if they catch you, the spirit of your father will help you," my friend said.

He left me alone near the edge of the camp, which was surrounded by barbed wire and armed guards. But the refugees were allowed to go outside the camp to gather fire wood in the forest. It was getting dark. People were walking back into camp with the firewood. I pretended I was one of them, and followed them in.

I felt so alone and full of fear, not knowing how to tell who was my friend or who was my enemy.

Beside a flowering tree (which in Khmer is called a *derm ongkea dai*), I found the big community well where people were coming to draw water. (I later thought of it as Jacob's well.) I was thirsty, but I didn't know how to get water. I asked for water. The people suspiciously questioned me.

"Do you have any relatives here?"

"Yes," I said. "I have an aunt here named Noy." Someone ran to find my aunt.

A tall guy, much bigger than I, who was wearing western clothes, walked up to me and intentionally bumped against me. I started and cringed, sure he was going to kill me.

"Tum!" the man said with amusement.

I looked at his face. It was my cousin, Thean, my aunt Noy's son. She had sent him to show me the way to her place.

The refugees were not free to go to the village or to the city of Aranya, except with a permission slip. And the guards were cruel. They beat people, persecuted the new refugees, and took their money. If you had no money, they'd take it from your relatives. My aunt was afraid to keep me.

I'm trapped, I said to myself. *I thought in Thailand I would find freedom.*

One of the guards was a distant relative of my aunt, and he had known my mom. Even though he was a cruel man, he decided to help me and gave me advice because he had liked my mom.

Without identification, I was in danger. A man named Pricha had just died two weeks earlier. He was my age. The photo on the dead man's I.D. card looked like me. His brother, named Mon, gave me Pricha's I.D. card, and that way he probably saved my life.

Pricha had escaped in the first exodus from my village, in 1975. Because he paid the guard, he was allowed to go to work outside the camp for a Thai farmer on the border. While working there, he was killed by the Khmer Rouge.

So I took his name, a Thai name meaning "Happy". I had to learn to answer to the name "Pricha" and give that name when asked.

With an I.D. I felt more safe. I began to look around; and I found, for the first time since the Communists took over, an opportunity to continue my education. Some refugees who knew French and English ran a private school, but I couldn't afford to go there. The Red Cross and the Catholic Charities ran a community center where they taught English one hour each day. The missionaries--John from America, along with Janet and Zella from England and Scotland-- were smart. They said they would teach me if I would help cook the soup and serve the orphans each day.

I heard a boy pray that first day I helped with the orphans. His name was Lam Vong. He prayed in the Thai language. He prayed to "the Lord Jesus".

What god is that? I wondered. This name was new to me.

91

Map #3

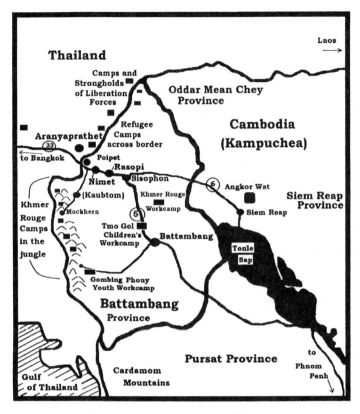

Battambang Province from 1975 to present

Pictured in map: (positions and names are approximate.)

Khmer Rouge Workcamp -- The Khmer Rouge evacuated the villagers to this dry, barren field (after a seven-day march) where they were starved and forced to do slave labor for "Angka", the organization.

Tmo Gol -- Children's Communal Workcamp where Physa was taken at age 14, worked, indoctrinated, starved. This camp was situated near the mass grave of a "killing field", where the KR left thousands of dead.

Youth Workcamp -- Near Pailin, Physa worked here two years, building a dam (called "Gombing Phouy") by hand.

Mockhern -- After the Vietnamese Communist takeover, the Khmer Rouge hid in the jungle, planting land mines, raiding villages, trading fire with liberation forces, and shooting refugees, many thousands of whom attempted to cross the border to refugee camps to escape persecution, starvation, and death. By logging and mining, the Khmer Rouge continue to purchase Thai and Chinese arms.

Kaubtom -- Physa's childhood village, now a ghost town. The Khmer Rouge demolished all family houses. Vietnamese Communists did not allow the villagers to return there, since it lay too close to KR strongholds, was heavily mined, and susceptible to Thai raids.

Nimet -- Vietnamese Communists placed the remaining 300 villagers here, further from jungle dangers, but in the line of fire between Khmer Rouge and liberation forces. From here, Physa was inducted into the new government's army and assigned to patrol the Thai border. He escaped to Thailand in August, 1979.

Physa's adopted sister was killed during a Khmer Rouge raid. After that, his mother and two sisters escaped to Thailand; Nimet was demolished; and the villagers ordered to start a "New Nimet", called Rasopi.

Aranyaprathet -- Refugee camp where Physa took the identity of a dead man and first heard of *the Lord Jesus*. He stayed there from August, 1979 to January, 1980.

Aranyaprathet, Thailand -- Town where Physa's mother, sisters, and their families live. Physa paid to get them out of the camp, and bought property for them to farm.

Rasopi -- New Village begun by the old villagers ,in the 1980's. Trees had to be planted and life is more difficult. Physa's brothers Nonglam and Soon farm rice near here.

I lived there three months, helped the missionaries, and learned a little English.

Announcements blared over big loudspeakers in the camp. When the refugees heard announcements, everyone hushed. One day, the announcement said there would be interviews for immigration to the United States. Khmer refugees were going to the USA, Canada, France, Belgium, Australia, and Brazil. I decided to try to go to the United States of America.

I thought, *I don't want to stay in this situation. But I can't go back home.* So I went for an interview.

The interviewer asked my name and wrote my new name in the English alphabet the way it sounded to him. He spelled it, "Physa." This is not an Asian spelling.

Many people didn't pass the interviews. I tried to give the right answers.

"Why do you want to go to America?" they asked.

"I want a better life," I answered.

"Are you really a legal refugee?" I showed my I.D.

"What will you do there?"

"I will go to school and I will work."

"If you go there, you have to stay there."

"Yes, I know. I will die there."

Refugees were required to go voluntarily. A month later, I received the news: I had passed! Catholic Charities paid the $350 for my transportation and I agreed to pay them back after getting a job in America. (A year later, I paid it off.)

My relatives and friends cried when I left.

Refugees chosen for immigration were taken by bus to Bangkok. On the way, I was amazed to see the prosperity of Thailand. It was January, and lights of many colors still adorned businesses and rich people's houses.

In Bangkok, we were locked in a jail-like cement building with security guards. It was very hot, with no air conditioning or fan. We were kept there two weeks.

Occasionally we were allowed to go onto the roof where we could see all of the city of Bangkok. I saw couples holding hands; students talking; vendors setting out food to sell on the street; bicycles, cars, normal life. Freedom!

Will I ever have a life like that? I wondered. I was nineteen years old.

At the Communist work camps, part of the Khmer Rouge propaganda was to teach us to fear white people. They told us that white people would eat us. Or else they would enslave us and make us work in their plantations.

I believed this. I thought my sponsor, whoever he was, would be my master and make me work in his plantation. This must be why he was bringing me to America.

Physa at age 19 in the Aranya Prathet refugee camp in Thailand, December, 1979, before he was taken to the Battaan refugee camp in the Philippines, January, 1980. This is the only photograph Physa has of his youth in Cambodia and Thailand.

PART 2

"You came near when I called you,
and you said,
'Do not fear.'"
(Lamentations 3:57)

7. The Man In White

At three o'clock in the morning, we were awakened. The same fear came over me that I had in the killing fields that it was my turn to be taken out in the night and killed. Would I just disappear? Would no one ever hear of me again?

But we later learned that they took us in the night so all 350 refugees could get through the Bangkok streets to the Navy cargo ship before the morning traffic started. The U.N. had sent a ship from the Philippines to get us.

We stood in line waiting to go on board. The sun rose. We were each given a cup of instant noodles. Called by name, one by one, the refugees boarded the ship. Underneath, where people slept, there were no windows and it was hot. At 3:00 or 4:00 p.m. the ship started moving. A smaller Philippine army ship escorted us. The Filipino soldiers carried orchids and other things they got in Bangkok. The soldiers looked like Khmer people to me, so I spoke to one.

"Brother do you know where the restroom is?"

He didn't understand. He answered in words I couldn't understand.

Hmmm. Here's a race that looks like me, but speaks a different language. Right then I felt an ambition to be their friend and speak their language.

The ship moved slowly, maybe twenty miles an hour. As we left Thailand, the Philippine soldiers did their routine military salutes to the Thai Navy. Never had I seen anything like that; also the sights along the coast, the commerce and activity. Then I was out on the ocean, a new experience for me. I saw lights on the water. I thought, *How do they do that? How do they get electricity out there?* Later I learned they use batteries.

We sailed out of the Thai Gulf, past Vietnam, and into the open sea. Out on the smooth water we saw dolphins, flying fish, and a school of tuna.

On the ship next day, a soldier dropped something overboard. He was lowered over the side into the water. Three soldiers on the deck aimed their M16's toward him.

Oh, they're going to shoot him. His mom won't know what happened to him, I thought.

But as we watched, he reached into the water to retrieve what had been lost, then he was pulled back up to safety and everyone clapped and cheered. The guns were lowered, and we learned that the guns were aimed for his protection, in case sharks came near.

A storm hit. People got sick. We were given pills for the sea-sickness, which made us sleepy. The refugees lay prostrate in the center of the ship, in long rows, with heads toward the outsides and feet toward the center, where a long isle separated the rows of people, sick and afraid of the stormy sea. We thought we were going to die. The refugees were praying to Buddha, to their ancestors, to any god they could think of.

Then I remembered what John, Janet, and Zella had told me.

"Whatever happens to you, ask the Lord Jesus; He will help you."

O Lord Jesus, I began to pray. *If you really are God, if you really have power, help me now.*

Then I slept; and I had a dream. In my dream, from where I lay I could see the calm sea and way out toward the east, where the sun was rising, I could see a form of a man walking on the water, coming from the east, all dressed in white, in what looked like Middle Eastern robes. His face was blurred.

I lay on one side, about half way down the long row of refugees inside the cargo ship. The man in white reached the boat and he stepped right up onto it, then walked inside, straight down the center isle, past the sleeping people. He didn't look at anyone else, but walked straight toward me, and stopped at my feet. He reached down his hand and pulled me up to a sitting position. He called me by name.

"Don't be afraid, Physa," the man in white said. "I will be with you."

When I awoke, I didn't think too much about the dream. I thought maybe he's one of the spirits or angels in which my culture believes. But immediately I noticed a change in my thinking. Usually my first waking thoughts were of fear and starvation and death. This morning I only thought, *I'm hungry. I want Asian food.* I longed for rice, fish sauce and peppers. I felt a new hope.

On the ocean, large commercial ships passed us going fast. They were red, green and black. As we drew close to the Philippine shore, small boats, islands, and coconut trees came in sight. I began to feel better, thinking *I'm not going to die afterall.*

From the harbor we saw factories along the shore. On land, as we traveled to the camp, I saw billboards for the first time in my life. I thought they were screens for movies like I used to see as a boy when people came into our village with Thai and Khmer movies to show the village people. I thought the pictures on the boards must be telling a story. Never before had I seen advertisements or commercials.

I saw people nicely dressed. I saw villagers, farm things, produce.

This is like home, I thought.

It was January, 1980. The construction of the refugee camp at Morong Bataan was not yet completed. It lay in a remote jungle area, surrounded by mountains and bamboo trees.

There was no barbed wire this time, though. Nearby lay farms, and a river.

At the camp white people from the U.N. and the Red Cross gave us steamed rice. We were not restricted. We were allowed to go out to the river to swim, to the village five kilometers away to buy fruit, and to the ocean ten kilometers away.

The villagers treated us kindly. When we bought fruit, such as bananas, they'd always add a little something extra as a gift.

During the rainy season, we could see a waterfall in the jungle, coming down from the mountains.

I stayed in that camp for seven months.

Refugees found ways to earn spending money. Some people wove baskets from vines they gathered in the forest. Those who were educated, taught classes. I had learned a little English at the Thai camp, so now I taught people the English alphabet, and though I didn't charge some students, others gave me maybe 20 pesos. So I had some loose change.

At the camp I met a Khmer man named Dara Pen, who was a Christian missionary. He had a Filipino wife and they had been sent as missionaries to the Philippines.

As a child, Dara had been orphaned, and missionaries in Kampuchea (Cambodia) adopted him. The American Embassy had gone out looking for educated Khmer people not connected with the government to work for them during the war. They hired Dara Pen. They took him to Washington, D.C. to work as a broadcaster for Voice of America. He also did speaking and taught French in a Bible College. He met his wife, Ligaya, in church. She had come as a student from the Philippines. Then they were sent back there in 1980 as missionaries.

In the refugee camp, English classes were announced.

"Please come to learn English and hear about Jesus."

I went and was given a Khmer Bible. I started reading it. When I read the part about Jesus walking on the water, then I knew the man I dreamed about on the boat was the Lord Jesus.

"In two weeks, we will have a baptism," announced the American and Philippine missionaries. I raised my hand that I wanted to be baptised. So I was given a copy of the book of John and told to read it.

I was tested on my knowledge of the Bible. The missionaries interviewed me.

"Why do you want to be a Christian?"

"I want to believe in the Lord Jesus."

"Are you sure you have the right reasons?"

"If I could cut my heart open and let you see what color it is, I would do that." (This was a saying of my people.)

I was baptised in the river. Later, few of the refugees who were converted in the camps stayed with the Lord. Only the good seed would remain.

I started going to church. But I was afraid people in the camp would make fun of me and say, "Oh, you are a child of Jesus." So I would hide my Bible in the bag I carried on my back.

One time it was too hot to meet in the building, so we met outside under a tree for church. I kept my Bible hidden. The preacher asked who had their Bible. I raised my hand. He thought I was lying. I took it out of my bag, ashamed. He lectured me about always having my Bible ready. After that, I didn't hide it.

Since my years in the Communist camps, I was afraid at night. I had a frightening, recurring dream that I was trying to escape to Thailand and someone was chasing me to kill me. The camp restrooms were not yet built, and we had to go out in the dark forest at night. I was very frightened that ghosts or something would get me in the dark. I would jump and run at the sound of a lizard crawling through the dry leaves.

"You can pray to God and He will take away your fear," the pastor said to me. So I asked God to take away my fear. Then I forgot about it. The next time I went out at night, I realized I wasn't afraid. That was the first prayer of my Christian life; and God answered it. He took fear from my heart and mind. One day I read Second Timothy 1:7. "For God has not given us a spirit of fear, but of power and of love and of a sound mind." (NKJV)

I taught classes daily. One of my students was a girl named Sareoum, who was very kind to me. She was the oldest child of her family and she helped care for the younger children. I liked her, so the second month I didn't charge her. Her father told me she liked me. I was invited to her home, where she cooked for me.

Khmer boys are taught never to touch a girl. And of course, her parents were watching us. Her parents didn't know any English. There was a blackboard. I pretended to be teaching her English.

"I like you," I wrote on the chalkboard.

"I like you, too," she wrote back.

Every day we walked to the river with some of Sareoum's siblings and friends.

Along the way, I picked wildflowers and gave them to her. She washed my clothes for me in the river, and mended them. We gave each other food, which is one way Khmer people show their affection and approval. We had our picture taken together.

"Son," her parents told me. "We like you. Just promise to keep the moral rules of Khmer culture. No sexual contact until marriage."

My clothes were tattered and worn. My cousin in Gardena, California found out where I was and sent me twenty-five dollars. I spent twenty dollars on a pair of jeans and tennis shoes. I was so happy; I felt like a millionaire.

One day my name was called. "In a couple of weeks we will call you again, and it will be time for you to go to America."

Happily I ran to tell my friend, Sareoum. She cried.

"Don't forget us," her mother said. They didn't know if they'd ever get out of the refugee camps.

On the day I was called, a gentle, cold rain was falling. Two or three buses of refugees were taken. My friend and I promised to write. I wanted to hug her. But I did not. It was the first time I ever cried over a girl.

On the bus, I sat near an open window in the back. Sareoum stood next to the bus, talking to me. The bus started. She followed the bus as far as she could, then she stood still, watching the bus leave, for as long as I could see.

Again, I felt alone and empty. It was like I lost something. But I heard a voice inside me that said, *The One in whom I put my hope, He is my best friend of all.*

8. I Meet My "Master"

In Manila, I wrote to my girlfriend. Then, on July 31, 1980 I took an airplane ride for the first time.

At the airport, we refugees saw automatic doors for the first time. Before we reached the doors, they opened out toward us, all on their own. We yelled and jumped back. Then we all laughed at each other.

Oh, this is what I used to read about as a kid, I thought on the plane.

Then I had to use the toilet. When I flushed it, the water came out green. *Oh, no.* I thought I did something wrong, and the airplane fuel was leaking.

Back in my seat, I pulled my blanket over my head. I didn't want anyone to know I was the one who broke the plane.

We stopped in Hong Kong for refueling and to my relief, the plane wasn't broken. Next we landed in Alaska to change planes, then we departed for San Francisco.

The flight attendants gave us food and treated us kindly. They had brown hair, blond hair, red hair. *Oh, these people are so beautiful,*

I thought. To me, they were like angels. But they spoke so fast, I couldn't understand what they said.

In the San Francisco airport, the refugees waited in line for more than two hours to process our refugee visas. I felt very thirsty. But I didn't have enough money to buy anything. I saw people drinking out of a fountain. They just bent over it and the water came out and they drank it. It must be free, I thought. I tried it. I bent over the fountain, but no water came out. I was afraid to try to ask how it worked. Then I watched other people more closely. When they stepped up to the fountain, I heard a click. Then I saw the pedal. I tried pressing the pedal with my foot. The water came out!

The San Francisco Bay and bridges impressed me. I saw nice cars and riches. I was filled with emotions--joy and fear at the same time. I felt joy to be in this new country, where everything was new and full of promise. But I also felt fear and uncertainty. I didn't know who was sponsoring me, or how he would treat me if I had to work as a slave in his plantation.

Lord, please let my master be a good person and treat me well, I prayed.

For three days we were kept at Hamilton Air Force Base, surrounded by a fence with gates that closed like a jail.

In the weather of the San Francisco Bay Area, the refugees shivered in our thin, worn clothing. A charity gave us a big pile of used clothes, and everyone grabbed whatever we could get our hands on. I found a sweater that fit me. I was small and skinny. It was a black sweater. No one told me it was a ladies' sweater. And when I wore it, it felt scratchy.

After three days and two nights, I was taken to the San Francisco airport and put on a plane to Los Angeles. I was sent into the plane with a note and told, "Your sponsor will be waiting for you there." I was alone. And I would soon meet my master.

But when I got off the airplane at Los Angeles, no one met me and I didn't know where to go. I still had five dollars in my pocket. I saw concessions selling hotdogs for two or three dollars. I was hungry, but what could I do? My five dollars didn't make me as rich as I thought.

`"Tum!" I heard a voice and turned around and there was one of my cousins, whom

I had not seen since 1975. He was my sponsor! What a relief. I was not going to be sold as a slave after all.

In the big parking lot, we got into my cousin Chai's Nissan car. We drove onto the big freeway. The artificial smell of the air freshener in the car, and fast driving on the freeway, made me feel sick. Since leaving the Philippines, I could not sleep; I had not adjusted to the time change; I had not eaten very much; I was cold.

When we reached my cousin's house in Gardena, my aunt, cousins, and other relatives were cooking a feast for us.

It was good to see family and eat familiar food. But I didn't feel good. And I didn't know what was going to happen to me.

9. New Life in America

"Don't worry. You'll go to school first," said my cousin, who was my sponsor in America. "And you'll get $250 a month from the refugee help fund and food stamps for the first six months."

It was summer when I arrived and moved in with my Cousin Chai in his rented house in Gardena, California.

The neighbors were throwing away an old bike and I asked for it. I fixed it, painted it, put new tires on it. In the fall, I rode it to school. No one told me it was a ladies' bike.

A couple named Mary Joelle May and John picked me up every Sunday in their green pick-up truck and took me to church. My aunt and cousin went along with me. The Jehovah's Witnesses and Mormons also came to the door. Some refugees would go with them because they didn't know the difference between Christian churches and cults.

At church they sang, "Victory In Jesus" and "Give me Oil in my Lamp". Those were the first Christian songs I learned.

Mary Joelle helped me get into the ESL program at the local high school. She talked to the principal, and even though I was older, he let me come to school with the high school students. I received free lunches. I worked nights at Virco Manufacturing for $3.50 an hour assembling tables, from 6:00 p.m. until 1:00 or 2:00 a.m.

When I first heard people say, "Are you *Cambodian?*" or "You come from *Cambodia.*" I did not understand.

"What is 'Cambodia'?" I asked. I had never heard that word before. In my language, I am "Khmer" and I am from "Kampuchea".

I did not understand American girls, either. One day I was riding my bike to school and three tall blond girls saw me and stopped me. They held my bike and took hold of me. They laughed at me.

"Give me your bike. It's a girls' bike. You shouldn't have it." They teased me. They could see I was afraid and one girl kissed my cheek. People were driving by. I was afraid someone would see. In my culture, I would be forced to marry a girl for touching her. I had never known girls who acted like this.

I needed help adjusting to this culture. Help came the next summer in the form of a young American couple named Mark and Viola Brown, who had sponsored my cousin as a refugee. They invited me to live with them for a few months. They were good people, and they took me to church with them. I paid $150 a month for my room and food.

Mark and Viola taught me many important things, like what movies to watch or not to watch, and what people to hang around with; and they helped me with the language. They took me on holidays to Redondo Beach and Santa Monica Beach--beautiful places.

The people in Mark and Viola's church treated me kindly. One day I was invited to a barbecue dinner in the backyard of the nice home of Richard, the pastor of the church. When we said good-bye, I wanted to express my gratitude and love.

"Brother, I love you," I exclaimed, giving the host a big hug. "You are so fat!"

That's a compliment to a Cambodian. But Mark and Viola explained to me later that in America those words are not a compliment, and I shouldn't say them to anyone.

I finished the ESL studies at the high school; and Mark and Viola bought a new home. I moved with them to help them with painting and landscaping. I took a welding class in trade school and got a job as a welder. After two years I was promoted to inspector of welding.

My Cambodian girlfriend, Sareoum, whom I had met in the Philippine camp was sponsored along with her family by people in Joilet, Illinois. She worked there as a waitress. She met there a man from my village in Cambodia, named Ta-Thong. He was the son of our village medium, who had tried to call forth the spirit of my father. They came to America before I did. He told Sareoum that the old man had become a Christian before he died.

For two years, Sareoum and I wrote to each other and talked on the phone regularly. Her mother wanted me to move to Illinois and marry her daughter. The time came when she didn't want to wait for me any longer. She said lots of guys were asking about her.

I talked to my friends.

"Don't go," Mark said. "Let her come here."

"Don't go," my church friends said.

"Don't go," my cousin said.

But I wanted to go, and I gave my boss two weeks' notice.

Lord, if it's your will, let me go, I prayed. *If it's not your will, then stop me from going.* But my heart wants to go and marry this girl.

It was two weeks before the Cambodian New Year, which occurs in April. I told Sareoum I'd come after the New Year. I bought an airline ticket to Illinois for a Thursday in April at 10:00 a.m. Then on the Saturday before my scheduled flight, I attended the Cambodian Festival in Long Beach.

At the festival, I met a man named Kean who had lived with me in the Philippine refugee camp. We were happy to see each other. I told him where I was going.

"Oh, my brother and sister live in Illinois, too," he said. "Do me a favor. My other sister is graduating from high school and she needs to go to Illinois where she can find a job. Will you take her there? She has a car and you can drive her there in her car."

"Are you sure? Wouldn't it be improper for us to be together like that?"

"It's okay. She's like a sister to you."

So I said I would do it. I called my girlfriend to tell her I would come two days later than planned, on Saturday. I gave up my non-refundable ticket. Then early Friday morning, my friend Kean called. He woke me up.

"Physa, I have to tell you. My sister changed her plan. She got a job here. She won't be going to Illinois."

Then it hit me. *It's from the Lord,* I thought. *He is stopping me as I asked Him to do. I must listen to Him.*

I called my girlfriend.

"Maybe I'll come in six months or a year." She was angry. She broke up with me and soon married someone else.

My loneliness caused me to think more about my family and all those I had left behind in Cambodia. I thought about them often, and prayed for them to become Christians.

Many young people my age had their minds mostly on material things. The desire for things consumed them. They wanted cars, clothes, and electronic things.

Besides missing my family and wanting to earn money to send back home to help them, I

117

was a normal youth. My friends and I would call each other. "Let's go have a picnic." Or, "Let's go fishing." Sometimes after church we cooked chicken soup and ate and talked.

The time my friends and I attended the Cambodian New Year's Festival, a group of Cambodian musicians performed on stage.

A Laotian acquaintance said, "That guy sings like someone I know."

"What's your friend's name?" I asked casually.

"Art," he answered. That got my attention. It was the name of my lost brother.

Art left our village home when I was a small boy, before 1975. He fled to Laos. Then Laos fell to Communism. He escaped to Thailand. Then he became a refugee to America. But I never heard what had happened to him, and did not know if he was alive or dead.

I was curious.

"Does this singer friend of yours have one eye bigger than the other?" I asked. "And does he have a scar over one eyebrow?" (From where he fell on the rock when my mom gave birth to him in the field.)

"Yes," my friend said. "That's him!"

"He's my brother! Where does he live?"

"He lives in San Francisco."

Mark and Viola and the church people gave me the money to go find my brother Art. So I drove to San Francisco with my friend.

Art had been the bad boy of the family, the fourth child born. When the third child died, he became the number three son. He didn't want to work on the farm. He ran away to the city. He brought back things from the city. Then he went to Laos to find our number one brother, Boun, who ran away from home in 1963. He also lived for a while with our grandfather's brother in Thailand, but during the war we lost contact with Art.

Now I was in San Francisco looking for Art. My friend and I found the high rise apartment building where we had been told Art lived, and climbing to the fifth floor, we found the number, and knocked on the door.

Art was there with Laotian friends, cooking pork and beef, smoking, and drinking beer. He had long hair. I spoke to him in the Laotian language. I told him I was his brother. He was stunned. He didn't recognize me. The last time he saw me I was a young boy.

119

To test me, he spoke Cambodian.

`"If you are my brother, what is your mom's name?" I answered in Cambodian.

"Oh, my brother!" Art exclaimed, convinced. In our culture crying shows weakness. He hugged me and patted my head, showing he's bigger. I spent the night. We talked a long time, then went out and rode the cable cars.

Physa's brother Art and his bride wearing traditional Cambodian wedding clothes for their traditional-style wedding in the mid-1980's in Long Beach, California. This is several years after Physa found him in San Francisco. He is the same brother who chased Physa as a boy.

I had other relatives in California--aunts, uncles, and cousins. My Aunt Noy became very ill with stomach cancer. She worshiped Buddha. She tried sacrificing a chicken to her ancestors. She only got worse. I gave her a Bible in the Thai language, which she had learned to read as a girl.

My aunt read the Bible. She let me pray with her and she gave her heart to the Lord Jesus. She took chemotherapy too, but I know the Lord touched her. She was healed completely.

Later, when I was about twenty-two I moved to Long Beach and worked as a welder with a different company.

I attended there a wedding feast in a Laotian-Cambodian home. My Christian friend was marrying a girl who attended the Baptist church with him. She said she was a Christian. The evening before the wedding, the bride's family had prepared the feast and invited about twenty Christian friends of the bride and groom.

The guys visited downstairs while the girls prepared for the wedding upstairs.

The bride's grandma still believed in spiritism. Out in the backyard, she killed a

121

chicken. She wanted to bring happiness to her granddaughter, so there in the backyard she called to the spirits of her ancestors and offered the sacrifice of the chicken to them. She asked them to come and bless the marriage.

None of us knew what the grandmother was doing. But suddenly we heard a scream from upstairs. We ran upstairs and found the bride trying to jump out the second story window. The groom and four men couldn't hold her. She cursed, used bad language, and tore her clothes uncontrollably.

The family quickly called for a sorcerer, whom they paid to get the spirit out of her. He tied a cotton string, considered to have magical powers, around her wrists and neck. With incantations he tried to force the spirit to go out through her hands or her mouth. He accomplished nothing. They called another sorcerer. He could not remove the spirit, either.

Then the Christians asked the parents of the girl, "Will you let us pray to the Lord Jesus? Will you believe?" The family were afraid of being shamed on the eve of their daughter's wedding, so they finally agreed to let us pray.

We removed the statue of Buddha and other false objects and idols from the house. We began to read out loud from the Bible about the miracle of the Lord Jesus at the wedding feast in Cana. The girl was still bound and writhing on the sofa. We kept reading scripture louder and louder.

The girl began to cry in a strange voice, "Oh, don't make me go back. Hell is too hot."

We told the spirit, "You have to leave. This body does not belong to you. Leave her, in the name of the Lord Jesus."

"I don't want to hear that name," the spirit pleaded.

"We command you to leave, in the name of the Lord Jesus."

The girl began to have seizures. Then she stopped and lay still as if dead. Someone called an ambulance and covered her with a blanket. She was okay.

On the wedding day, the grandmother gave her heart to the Lord and was baptised. The bride, Thong Lien, became a commited Christian. The groom, Hom, (called Brian) now serves as a board member in his church in Long Beach, California.

10. A NEW KIND OF VILLAGE

Many of the people of my childhood village in Cambodia became refugees to America and lived in Long Beach, California.

In the early 1980's, Christian people in Long Beach invited the refugee children to Sunday school. Then, the Laotian-Cambodian adults became interested and began attending a Sunday school class started for them at the church.

The English-speaking American church supported this growing ministry by calling Rev. Randy Beckum and his wife Lori to pastor the Southeast Asian people. Randy had just graduated from seminary, and this was his internship.

I first attended a Wednesday night Bible study at the home of Anong Hnim, who served as Randy Beckum's interpreter.

"We need helpers and leaders," said Randy. I felt the Lord leading me to volunteer to help.

First I helped teach the people to sing Christian songs and hymns. I sang, then they sang after me. We formed a choir and I became the director.

I was given a key to the church building. On my day off from work, I would go to the church and practice on the piano.

"Dear Lord, I pray and I ask that you will give me a knowledge of this instrument so I can use it to worship you." I prayed with great desire.

I couldn't afford music lessons, and I had no one to teach me, but I practiced and practiced for hours and hours. I used my ear. The tunes and harmonies began to come through my fingers on the keys.

I saved money from my paycheck and bought an electric guitar--a Yamaha, for $120. I used chord books to learn how to play. Then we had our own instrumental music as well as singers, which we used in special services.

Pastor Randy encouraged me to witness and share my testimony. I brought some people I knew to church with me. I read the Bible and Christian books to increase my knowledge of the Christian life.

Many of the people preferred to speak the Laotian language, which I also had learned orally. But I wanted to be able to teach these people from the Bible, so I bought books and taught myself to read and write Laotian, with the help of a man who taught me the alphabet and pronunciations. Laotian and Cambodian are completely different languages, though the characters of the two alphabets do look similar.

So I could better witness to Thai people also, whose language I spoke, I learned to read and write Thai as well.

In the summer of 1985 I had the opportunity to go to the Billy Graham Crusade in the Angel Stadium in Anaheim, where I helped as a counselor. Many Southeast Asian people came forward to pray each night. There I met Paul Ellison from the Christian and Missionary Alliance church. He told me his grandfather had been the first missionary to Cambodia and he had translated the Bible into the Cambodian language.

Paul spoke fluent Cambodian. He gave me his card and asked me if I would like to study with him in CMA Bible college extension classes he was teaching. I took these classes for two years and received the CMA church's diploma of theological studies.

However, I joined the Church of the Nazarene. There, I helped train teenaged Cambodians to participate in church services.

At this time, back in Cambodia, the second communist regime, who were Vietnamese, and the Cambodians who joined with them (supported by the Russians), weren't as bad as the Khmer Rouge. They did allow people to have property, use currency, and to work their own farms. But the Khmer Rouge Communists, now deep in the jungle, and the liberation army near the border, would get hungry and raid villages.

In 1984 I sent my uncle in Thailand $200 to give my mom. She spent half of it. Then one night about thirty guerrillas raided the village. They stole my mom's money. They raped women; they shot people; they burned houses, including my number five brother's house.

In these days my mom was raising an orphan girl who had been adopted by my brother, the Vietnamese Communist Army officer.

On that dark night of the raid, when my brother's house was burning, it was lighting up the village, making it hard for people to run and

127

hide from the soldiers. My sister took the hand of the little adopted sister and ran across the road with her to try to reach a hiding place. She pulled the little girl behind her. A raiding soldier with a gun saw them. He aimed at them and shot the little girl in the back. She crumpled and my terrified sister let go and ran for cover.

The soldiers shot the little girl again to make sure she was dead and left her lying on the muddy ground. It was flood season when the river overflows its banks and water covers the land, bringing fish and crabs everywhere. When the soldiers left, my mom came out of hiding and found the little girl. Crabs were crawling on her body, eating at her face and the flesh of her open wounds.

My mother described this event to me later. She grieved over the child. She chose to believe that the little girl was given to her so that her grown daughter's life would be saved. For if she hadn't been in the way, the soldier's gun would have killed my sister.

After that, my mom and her two daughters, Naiang and Pheny (and Pheny's husband), escaped across the border to Thailand. My brothers Nonglam and Soon stayed with their families in Cambodia. Boun, also married and living in Phnom Penh, retired from the communist army in 1986.

My mom and sisters found that there were no longer any protected refugee camps. After 1986, few refugees were allowed to come to America. Cambodian refugees in Thailand were forced to fight in the liberation army. They were kept like prisoners in a camp.

In front of Angkor Wat, 1980, after Physa escaped. Physa's siblings still living with their mother in Cambodia, left to right: Nonglam, the adopted sister (who was later killed), Naiang, Phenny, and a friend.

The Liberation Army controlled the camp, and they forced the boys and men in the camp to fight with their guerrillas for control of the country. My brother-in-law would have to fight.

To get my family out of danger, I worked hard in California and saved enough money to send $600 to my cousin in Thailand so he could hire someone to sneak my family out of the camp. Then I sent $1500 so they could have ID made for them, which made them Thai citizens.

Later, while living in Visalia, I would work and send my mom $800 to buy a four-hectare plot of land so she could have a rice farm to support herself; then $2,000 for her to build a house for herself and her daughter, son-in-law, and grandchildren.

During the growing season, they work the farm. During the off season, they work in factories in the city. My mom stays home and cares for the children while her adult children make the living. Near her home she grows mango, banana, and coconut trees.

I dreamed of one day going back to Cambodia and starting a village where the Christian Church would stand at the center of the village instead of a Buddhist temple.

In Thailand, 1984, shortly after leaving the refugee camp: Physa's mother and his younger sister Penhy. His mother is holding Penhy's first child. The two older children are relatives.

Physa's fourth brother, Nonglam, gathering the cut rice stalks on his farm in Cambodia.

Buddhist festival for the spirits of the dead. Above, Soon and his family with gifts presented to the Buddhist monks. The festival includes incense burning and chanting, so the spirits of dead relatives will receive the gifts and merit will be won. There is much socializing, food for everyone, and music played on traditional Cambodian instruments. Below, Nonglam stands on far right with his family.

130b

Instead of worshiping false spirits in rebellion against God, we would worship the Lord Jesus in spirit and truth. People would learn the Bible and live by the faith and teaching of the Lord Jesus, rather than chanting rituals in a language they don't understand, appeasing false gods, and trying to earn merits in the vague hope of a better future life.

The English-speaking church in Long Beach provided our Laotian-Cambodian Christian community with a new spiritual center. Pastor Randy Beckum gave us vision and hope and a bridge between us and the English-speaking church. He was an encourager and he saw things before they happened. He even helped us find our own building and raise the money to pay for it!

We found a building on Anaheim Street, right in the center of the Laotian-Cambodian area of the city. The facility cost $450,000. The American church raised offerings to help us purchase the building. Most of the Laotian and Cambodian people were unemployed; but the Lord helped us raise $20,000!

Pastor Randy took us to English-speaking American churches in the area to hold services.

At these services, I gave my testimony. I told the story of how God preserved my life during the wars in Cambodia and brought me safely out of the killing fields; how the Lord Jesus revealed himself and his truth to me; how he had been teaching me and helping me to adjust to a different culture; and I shared about my desire to serve God with all my heart.

At first, I was scared to get up and speak in front of the people, afraid of their reactions. But as I obeyed the Lord, and began to speak from my heart, I felt the Spirit of God anointing me. I felt His power working through me.

I learned to keep giving and giving of myself as God gave opportunity. As I shared what He gave to me, He kept giving me more. More insights, more opportunities, more energy, more resources. The Lord always fed me, both spiritually and physically. This attitude of not holding on to anything, not being self-protective, became the attitude of my life. Once my spirit had nearly been broken by starvation, hatred, and killing. Now God filled me with hope and joy. He made me a happy man.

Before I was saved, I had a rebellious heart. God took out the rebellion. Now God's Spirit lived in me.

Before I escaped the destitution of Communist Cambodia, I thought if only I could reach Thailand, I could get things, riches, then I could be happy. I dreamed of owning five pair of jeans, four or five thousand baht (Thai money), and a new bicycle. In Thailand, I saw rich people, and I craved the things they had: good cars, good jobs, and nice homes.

But when I gave my heart to the Lord Jesus, even though I needed many of these things and I asked God to supply my needs, he gave me a satisfied heart--a heart that is satisfied with what he gives me. I found true riches in the Lord Jesus. And I wanted to tell others.

After I shared in the services, our choir sang. Then Randy preached. At each church we visited, we took offerings for our new church building. Finally, we raised enough money and moved into our new facility. We even had choir robes.

Other leaders contributed greatly to establishing this church, through their witness

133

and works. Two of those men were Pastor Anong Hnim and Pastor Prasaan Keoganoke.

The Beckums were called to be missionaries in a foreign field. Steve and Judy Ratliff came to be our pastor. They were very gifted people.

"We should train you to be a pastor and give you a preacher's license," Rev. Ratliff said to me.

I took Bible College extension classes from Dr. Cliff Fisher. In 1987, I finished the Course of Study for Ministers.

Friday nights I helped the youth pastors, Brian and Alan, teach young people, and Saturdays I practiced with the choir. Then in 1989, God called me to be a pastor.

Dr. Steve got leukemia and had to leave. Then Dr. Brent Cobb came to be our pastor. His friend Leon Hendricks pastored a church in Visalia. Rev. Hendricks telephoned Dr. Cobb.

"We have Laotian people coming to our church who need a pastor who can speak their language," he said.

"We have a Laotian-Cambodian man who has the fire of God in his heart," Brent Cobb answered. "And he wants to preach."

He took me to Visalia. I preached for the Laotian people there. They asked me to be their pastor. They presented to me this proposal:

They would pay me five-hundred dollars a month plus housing. The Central California District would pay my health care. This proposal was very low. I worked at that time as a welder and was paid more than $2,000 a month. Taking such a cut in pay would be hard for me. But I wanted to be a pastor. And I knew it was a work of faith.

"Will you come?" they asked.

I prayed and fasted for two weeks. After working at welding all day, I went to bed at night very tired. But one night at one o'clock I felt someone shake me awake.

"Physa, wake up," I heard an urgent voice rousing me.

I opened my eyes, and in a blink I saw a person in white; then they disappeared. Jumping out of bed, I knelt and prayed for my family, and all I could think to pray about. My spirit was in an urgency of praying.

Two weeks later, I heard from my mom.

"Your brother was shot," she told me.

She said my second brother, Soon, sneaked over to Thailand to buy things he needed on the black market. The Khmer Rouge found him in the jungle. They shot and wounded him and took all his money and the medicine he had bought. They held a gun to his head.

"Should we kill him?"

"No," they decided, leaving him lying in the jungle. The Thai border patrol found him and took him to a Thai hospital, where his wound and broken leg were treated.

When I heard the date when he was shot and nearly killed, I got goose bumps. It was the very time when I was awakened from sleep to pray.

"Can you send any money?" my Mom asked. I sent $400.

11. The Aliens in Your Midst

O Lord, I prayed, *which place should I go? I want to be in the center of your will.*

Before receiving the call from the Nazarene Church in Visalia, I had received an offer from an Alliance church in Attleboro, Massachussetts.

The Alliance church had many candidates. The Nazarene Church in Visalia had no other candidate, no other qualified Cambodian-Laotian minister.

I had a dream. I saw people hungry and skinny, like the people in the Khmer Rouge Communist work camps. They wanted food. They desperately needed to eat. Then I awoke.

These people need to be fed the Word of God, I thought.

I gave away my furniture and everything I owned except my red Nissan Sentra, some clothes, one pot for cooking rice and another pan for stir frying. The church people in Visalia offered to help me move.

"I don't need help," I told them. "All I own is two pots for cooking."

A woman named Pearl had a farm with walnut trees on which stood a rentable mobile home trailer, which she offered to me. I moved in. Pastor Hendricks came to see me in the trailer.

"Is this really all you have? Just two pots?" he asked.

"You remind me of myself when I graduated from seminary and took my first pastorate. Only you have even less than I had."

He knelt and prayed with me.

Rev. Hendricks made an announcement on Sunday and people brought me pots and pans, towels and other things.

"Oh, it's too much," I said.

Later, I wanted to be closer to the people and to the church, so I rented a small apartment for $275 from Inez Cox. I lived there a long time.

I was ordained as an elder in the Church of the Nazarene In 1991 by General Superintendent Dr. Eugene Stowe. Dr. Will Spaite, the District Superintendent, appointed me to be the Southeast Asian coordinator for the Central California District.

Ministering to Southeast Asian refugees carried many challenges. The Laotian people in the Visalia church all lived on welfare, and had little earned income. God called me to give these people the gospel, though, and many were saved.

When I arrived, three Laotian families--about fifteen people--attended the English-speaking church. I prayed. We drove a van. Many more began coming. Some people came as a result of the compassionate ministries program--distribution of clothes, rice, and other food. Soon we had a large group of Laotian families, and we began meeting separately--worshiping, preaching, and teaching in the Lao language.

One young man named Lovan-Cheou came to the Lord Jesus, quit drinking and smoking, and took leadership training from me for four years. He was ordained, and he later took over the work in Visalia when I left.

Some of the people did not stay with the faith, because of the influence of the American culture, and because of the strong pull of the Buddhist temple.

His calling, gifts, and graces recognized by the church, Rev. Physa Chanmany receives ordination as a minister of the gospel, April 1991. Physa stands fourth from the right, in a class of ordinands and their spouses. Dr. Eugene Stowe is on the left, and Dr. Will Spaite is on the right.

The Laotian people who came to the Visalia church while Physa was ministering there. Physa baptised about half of these people.

I was disappointed by this, but the Lord reminded me of his own ministry. Even though he performed miracles, many people did not believe. He also spoke to me through the parable of the sower in Luke chapter eight. Not all of the seed falls on good soil.

Some of the people showed little spiritual commitment. One family said they became Christians in the refugee camp, but their lives did not demonstrate faith. These people held on to the things of the world.

When I first read the Ten Commandments as a young Christian, they stuck in my heart. For some of my people, that did not happen. They still held on to idols. In my culture, people reverence and worship many "sacred" objects.

When I became a Christian, I looked at the false "sacred" object I owned, and I said, *I shouldn't have this now.* And I threw it away.

Sadly, many new Christians look at the object of false worship they own and they say, "I shouldn't have this now. *Here, I will give it to my brother.*"

This is not true repentance and turning from idols. "You shall have no other gods before me."

I made mistakes in that early ministry. I did too much social work. I went to the hospital to interpret for the people. I went to court to interpret for them. I got too involved helping them. And they took advantage. Some people came to church just to get my help.

Too often, these people see the church as a place to receive. In the refugee camps, Christians gave them food and Bibles. They come to expect to be given things. This is how they see the church. I am teaching them that *we* are the church, and that what we receive, we have to give back. I tell them that as Christians, we are called to give to the strangers, the poor, the refugees. It is our duty. "Do not mistreat an alien or oppress him, for you were aliens in Egypt." (Exodus 22:21)

Though some refugees only come to the church in order to receive tangible help, they do hear the gospel. "And this gospel of the kingdom will be preached in the whole world as a testimony to all nations, and then the end will come," is written in Matthew 24:14.

"Why is your church not growing financially?" the mother church asked me. "We want you to become independent. The Laotian work is a burden to us."

I tried to explain to them that the Laotian population in that city was not large, and the Buddhist temple was strong. I told them that the people's response was God's work; my responsibility was to evangelize.

I was also busy working to supplement my small salary, and going to school. And to add to my responsibilities, I drove every month to Modesto and Merced to train Laotian and Cambodian leaders in those churches.

In Modesto, a strong Laotian congregation was paying the mother church $200 a month; but problems developed between them and the English-speaking church. The Laotian people left that church and started attending the Salvation Army and Baptist churches. The Cambodian people there organized a Church of the Nazarene. The Laotian people in Merced found a church home at the Salvation Army.

I'm glad I could help train those people and that they are going to churches that feed them the Word of God, and not back to the Buddhist temple, as some have done.

Besides the Buddhist influence, many refugees are deceived by Western culture.

In Eastern cultures, the devil looks ugly, evil. The people recognize him and fear him. But in this culture, sometimes the devil comes looking beautiful and enticing. The people coming here from eastern cultures may not recognize him.

"This thing is so nice, so beautiful; it can't be of the devil," the people think. (Read Ezekiel 28:12-19.)

Here in America, violence and killing is glorified. Evil is considered fun and entertaining (for instance, in many television programs, Halloween celebrations, etc.).

The Lord Jesus said, "You belong to your father, the devil, and you want to carry out your father's desire. He was a murderer from the beginning, not holding to the truth, for there is no truth in him. When he lies, he speaks his native language, for he is a liar and the father of lies." (John 8:44)

We must learn to recognize the devil and his lies.

In this culture, my people find so many choices. In their rural Asian culture, there was only one way, one lifestyle, one set of values shared by the entire village, and that was it.

I don't want to fail in my ministry to show the Southeast Asian families how to be Christian families, and how to train their children in the home. Here, they can no longer let their children run freely as in their villages back home. They cannot trust the surrounding community to teach their children the same values and lifestyles that they want for them.

So I visit in the homes in the evenings and gather the families around me to show parents and children how to talk with each other, how to read the Bible together, how to pray together.

If it is a challenge for Southeast Asian refugees to adjust to Western culture and fit into the American church (because of language, cultural, economic, and educational barriers), it is perhaps equally challenging for the English-speaking American church to make a place for these people whom God is bringing to them.

The American church likes having the refugee and cultural-minority people when they first come, and there are only a few of them. But they don't know what to do with these cultural groups when more and more of them respond to the love of Christ and the light of the gospel and their numbers increase; when they can no longer be contained in a classroom; when they need preaching in their own language, and they need to worship and fellowship together as a community of believers.

Often these works begin with the children: child evangelism in refugee and minority neighborhoods, other social work by Christians, busing the children in to VBS and Sunday School. Then the children want to keep coming and beg their parents to bring them, and soon adults are coming under the influence of the gospel and giving their hearts to the Lord Jesus. This has provided exciting missionary work and a fertile field for the gospel for the few Christians who have gotten involved sponsoring refugees, helping these new communities make adjustments, teaching English as a second language, and bringing the children to Sunday School.

Some English-speaking American churches are aging and their children's departments are dwindling. When these refugee and minority groups within the churches grow, they tend to be young families with many small children. If the majority of the children in the church are from minority-language and refugee families, the church has a big challenge. These children's parents are still learning to speak English. Some of them are not even literate in their own tribal languages. And while they are eager, they are still learning Christian truths like children, themselves. They don't have the ability or confidence to teach their own children, who are speaking and learning in English and becoming acculturated through the public schools.

In many cases, in fact, the children are serving as interpreters for their parents in the hospital clinics, schools, and the social service offices. This makes the parents feel they have less authority to give advice to their children.

In the churches, the English-speaking church people bear the burden of teaching the minority-language children, trying to assimilate the teens, and sharing facilities with the adults who need to worship separately in their own language.

I have noticed that as long as the minority-language, refugee people remain a minority, they just hide there (probably in a back room somewhere). But when they become the majority, attitudes change. When they become a large and active group, but unable to support themselves as a church, financially, the English-speaking church begins to consider them a burden.

Then the mother church gets in too much of a hurry to make the minority-language congregation independent, before they are fully trained in churchmanship, leadership, and the Word; before they are financially capable of independence; before they have adequate facilities; before they have developed a vision that can hold them together and carry them into the future.

The Long Beach First Church of the Nazarene is a good model. This mother church didn't set a limit of two or three years for the Laotian-Cambodian congregation to become independent. They gave them time. It took more than ten years. During that time, the mother church provided pastoral leadership, taught the children and youth, shared their facilities, and helped raise funds for the Laotian-Cambodian congregation to buy their own building.

Now the Laotian-Cambodian church worships in their own building, and have all their own adult leaders and pastors. The English-speaking mother church still gives some financial assistance and sends teachers on Sunday mornings for children and youth.

The Laotian-Cambodian church has two separate worship services: one for the older adults in their native Lao language, and one for the youth in English.

Early on, the mother church commited themselves to nurturing this Southeast Asian work along, helping them toward independence, patiently and lovingly and steadily. Their commitment has paid off in growth and health both for the Lao-speaking church and for the English-speaking church.

Personally, I am commited, and I am giving my life, to training future leaders of the Laotian and Cambodian churches. It will take time and perseverence. It will take at least a few individuals in the mother churches who believe in this work and who will support it and help the leaders of the English-speaking church to understand my people: their grieving over the painful experiences that brought them to America; their loss of a homeland; their difficult challenges with language and with cultural and economic survival; but also, their great joy in being found by Christ; their love of worshiping and learning together; their gratitude toward the English-speaking church for teaching their children.

I know the mother churches have financial constraints. Often they are giving generously to support world missions; but giving to and helping the aliens, the minorities who are your neighbors is a "hands-on" mission. I hope the general and district levels of denominations who assign missions budgets to local churches will decide to give budget credit to churches who are involved in these direct mission works.

I believe with the loving and patient support of the mother churches, future generations of these people will in fact grow to become integrated and one with the American church.

Physa, above right, training a class of ministerial candidates, who were leaders in Cambodian and Laotian churches in Modesto, Visalia, and Merced. The classes combined worship and fellowship with biblical and theological studies.

The training class (below) visiting a military base with Phil Carr (third from left) an Air Force navigator who attended Physa's classes. Physa stands second from right. Standing fifth from right is Bouphet Sidavong, who later pastored a Salvation Army Laotian church.

Pastor Physa (right and below) conducting a baptism service at Three Rivers, near Visalia, California.

149b

12. "Come and Teach Us"

When the district of the church in which I was ministering moved me to Fresno, I moved further from my former village family and friends who lived in Long Beach. I was excited about a new challenge, though. I was paid $700 a month plus rent. I lived in a three bedroom home.

The Rev. Sharon Stanley, a leader in refugee work in Fresno, helped me--and pastors in other denominations--to become acquainted and involved with many refugees in the Fresno.

In trying to start a Cambodian work in Fresno, I brought two Cambodian families to church with me. But these people were not trainable as leaders.

While I tried to establish a Cambodian Christian work in the city of Fresno, I had a part-time job working in the post office at night, sorting mail.

One day I received a letter from a lady named Eloise Powell in Santa Rosa, California. She said she was teaching a Sunday School class of Laotian people and helping them with English. She was attempting to give them the gospel; but it was difficult to overcome the language barrier.

"Will you come and visit these Laotian people in Santa Rosa?" Mrs. Powell pointedly asked me in her letter. I put the letter away and didn't answer. I believed God had called me to work in the Fresno area. Later, I received a phone call from this same lady.

"Will you come and preach to the Laotian people here in Santa Rosa?"

"Okay, I'll come one Sunday to preach to them. Bring all the Laotian people together. Have a potluck, because they will come if there is food." I drove there for three hours, north of San Francisco, and preached to the group of Laotian people in the city of Santa Rosa.

"We're going to pray that God will bring you to us," Mrs. Powell said.

"I'm busy in Fresno," I answered.

Mrs. Powell wrote to me again asking if I could find someone else to come help them.

Meanwhile the Cambodian people in Fresno were not responding to my efforts. The Alliance church already had a Cambodian ministry established in that city.

I continued to work in the Post Office. I had to redirect mislaid mail. One or two times a night I would see mail addressed to "Santa Rosa". Finally I took notice. *Maybe the Lord wants me to help them find a pastor,* I thought.

I called Mrs. Powell.

"If you want a pastor, come up with what you can pay. Go to the church board."

She sent me a budget of $1,000 a month from the American church, $100 a month from individual donors, and $100 from the Laotian people's offerings. So it was $1200 a month. I talked to the Laotian-Cambodian Christian leaders I knew. I tried to help the Santa Rosa church find a pastor for the Laotian people. I asked the newly-ordained pastor in Visalia, Sorsenginh, if he was interested; but he declined. No one I knew wanted to leave their community and go to Santa Rosa.

Working in the Post Office, I kept seeing mail for "Santa Rosa." I began to think, *Maybe God wants* **me** *to go there.*

I called Mrs. Powell again.

"Can you do more?" I asked.

152

Mrs. Powell just answered, "I'm praying you'll come."

Then I had a dream. I was walking in a field near a jungle. I saw three Asian men dressed in African dress coming down from a mountain. They were singing in a language I didn't understand. They had beautiful voices.

"Oh you guys, you sing so beautifully," I exclaimed. "It would be wonderful if you would come to church with me and sing Christian songs."

"Oh, if you come and teach us, we'll sing Christian songs," they answered.

I thought about what the dream could mean. I thought of the Laotian people in Santa Rosa. Those people come from a mountain area of Laos. They speak a tribal language that I don't understand. The African dress, what is that? Africa is where many missionaries are sent. A missionary! Did this mean God wanted me to go to be a missionary to the refugee community of Lao tribal people in Santa Rosa?

I drove again to Santa Rosa to visit. The people had no singing, no music, no instruments of their own. They had no youth group, no worship service; only a Sunday

153

school class with no commitment to the church at all. I thought, *These people really need to be taught the words of God in their own language.*

I knew God was calling me.

Some of the first Laotian Christians in Santa Rosa, California, 1994. Eloise Powell, their teacher, is third from left.

Learning to worship the Lord Jesus, play musical instruments, and sing Christian songs. Physa is second from left, at the piano. Santa Rosa, 1999.

Some of the Laotian Christians in Santa Rosa after church on Sunday June 6, 1999. Pastor Physa stands second from left, with his wife, Rachelle.

13. God Gives Me a Wife

I told God I had three criteria for a wife: "First Lord, she has to love you. Second, I have to love her. Third, she has to love me back."

There was a girl in Long Beach. We loved each other. But she didn't love God. Another girl loved God, and I loved her; but she didn't love me.

I had prayed for a wife since I was twenty-five.

In 1996, when I was thirty-six, I saw Pastor Dara Pen, the man who had led me to the Lord. He lived in Hacienda Heights, California. He attended the Cambodian church there, and his wife attended the Filipino church.

"You don't have a wife yet?" he said to me. "I'll pray for you to find a wife."

Later he telephoned me. "I found a girl in my wife's church. She is very gentle. Her family is Christian. She helps with the children. Come to visit me and I'll take you to church there so you can meet her. I'll introduce you to her."

This girl's name was Rachelle. Her family invited me and my friend to their house for

155

Filipino food. When I talked to Rachelle, her face glowed.

My friend Dara told Rachelle's parents, "Physa's looking for a wife. Let's leave them alone." The other adults and siblings left us alone in the room.

"How old are you?" Rachelle asked me. "Are you twenty-five?" She didn't believe me when I told her I was thirty-six, so I got out my I.D. to show her.

"Are you really a pastor?" she asked, seeing I was dressed casually in jeans and a sport shirt. She asked me all about my life. I told her funny stories about my adjustments to America. She laughed and cried.

Rachelle's family was Catholic in the Philippines. Rachelle read the Bible as a child and the Lord revealed His truth to her.

Her father, Ray, is a mechanical engineer. After they came to America, Rachelle and her mother, Rose, attended an evangelical church with a relative. They experienced God in a new way and they were changed deep in their hearts. Rachelle's father opposed the family's new walk of faith at first. Then he was also converted.

Listening to her talk, I was convinced she loved the Lord. I asked for her address and she wrote it on a napkin for me .

Back home in Santa Rosa, I wrote to her parents and asked permission to ask her out. In my culture you do that to show respect.

At first they laughed, then they decided, "He's respectful. He's not Americanized in that way. That's good."

I visited her again the following month, bringing fruit and flowers to her.   We drove together to Santa Monica. On the tree-lined path along the Santa Monica beach, Rachelle and I sat on a bench, talking.

I noticed someone quite a distance away, pushing a wheelchair toward where we sat. I turned to speak to Rachelle, and it seemed like only seconds later, I turned back around and there was the wheelchair right beside me.

How did it get that far so quickly? I wondered. An East Indian-looking woman pushed the chair in which an elderly woman sat, quietly smiling. I spoke to her, asked her a few general questions.

The old woman in the wheelchair told me that she had two sons; one son was a doctor in the United States and one was a teacher in Israel. I asked how old she was.

"Oh, you don't want to know," she answered, with a mysterious tone in her voice. "I'm very old!"

"But what about you?" she asked me. "How old are you?" I told her my age--thirty-seven.

"Are you married?" she asked. "No? Why wait so long?"

I didn't quite know what to say, with Rachelle sitting by my side.

"What about her?" the old woman pointed to Rachelle. "She would make a lovely wife for you."

I blushed and looked at Rachelle. The Indian woman pushed the wheel chair on. A few seconds later we turned toward the departing wheelchair--and we couldn't see it anywhere!

"Where is she?"

The path was open and visible a long ways in both directions. Behind us lay a busy street which would take some time to cross. How could anyone, especially an old woman in a wheelchair, disappear so quickly?

Rachelle and I both got goosebumps.

And after that, I listened to Rachelle more closely.

When Rachelle's employer sent her to a sales convention in San Francisco, she called and let me know the date. I asked if I could take her sightseeing after work.

"Okay," she said.

"I'll take you out to eat then," I said. We drove around the city. We talked until 11:00 at night. After that, we talked on the phone often.

One day I told Rachelle that I loved her very much and I wanted to marry her, with permission from her parents. She agreed.

She loved God. She loved me. And I loved her! We were married in the Santa Rosa church on December 27, 1997.

Rev. Physa and Rachelle Chanmany, May, 1999.

Love Made in Heaven

(dedicated to my beloved wife, Rachelle, without whose love

my life would not be complete)

Love is a feeling
Love is an emotion
Love is a commitment
Love is happiness
Love is a promise kept
Love is giving and sharing
Love is receiving
Love is forgiving.

To have love and to know true love
is to know God
and to understand His wisdom.
Love is flawless because
it is made in Heaven.
Love is the key to unlock the door
of the human heart.
Love is the highway to heaven
on which the Creator
calls us to walk
with His only begotten Son.

-- Physa Chanmany

14. Wings To Fly

Twelve years after I left Cambodia and Thailand for the United States, I returned to visit my mother and sisters in Aranya Prathet, on the Thai-Cambodian border. It was 1991. The Church in Visalia, in which I was ministering at the time, gave me a leave to go.

The plane landed in Bangkok and I stayed for two days in that great city of seven-million people. The third day, I boarded a bus and took a four-hour ride through the country. As the bus sped toward my destination, I observed every detail: fishing nets and farmers harvesting rice in their fields; farms big and small in the distance; coconut, banana and mango trees along the highway. Far across the rice paddies lay ponds and small lakes. Young boys watched over water buffalo and cared for the herds of cattle.

From the moving bus, I saw tall grasses dancing in the wind across the fields. Beautiful wildflowers bloomed along the highway. Far away, trees covered green mountains.

O Lord, I thought, *it is so beautiful and new, as if your mighty hand has just painted this picture of nature a day before I arrived here.*

Then the cool breeze of January blew gently through the window onto my face. I took a deep breath and said to myself, *I am really here again!*

In that moment a picture flashed back into my mind from my childhood: I had climbed into a tree to keep watch over our cows and oxen in the field. I looked out from my high perch and saw an eagle flying. I found myself wishing that I could fly and see the world from the eagle's view.

In the bus, remembering that childhood wish, it seemed like the Spirit of God opened my eyes and the words of a poem came to me. I saw that God had indeed given me wings. He had lifted me out of the killing fields. He had brought me out to the knowledge and faith of the Lord Jesus Christ. He had even allowed me to fly high over the continents and oceans in an airplane, to unknown places of which I had never dreamed.

The bus arrived in the Aranyaprathet station at one o'clock in the afternoon. My brother-in-law was there to meet me. He took me to my mother's home.

The family had cooked a meal of fishes and chicken. They also prepared the Cambodian farm dish with wild vegetable salad called *Teouk Greoung.*

It was good; the first time in a very long time that I had eaten a meal in my mother's home.

In my heart I prayed for my mother and my siblings, for I long to have the permanent reunion with them and the Lord, which is the eternal reunion.

He Gives Me Wings

Even though I'm poor, I'm very rich
because I walk with the Most High.
In the time of trial and tribulation,
when I am weak, He makes me strong.

War, sickness, hunger and separation
are parts of human lives.
In the time of war, I saw
the strong become weak,
and the weak become strong.
Men's wisdom brought them to destruction.

When I seek the face of my Creator,
He puts me on the path of love,
understanding, righteousness, and peace.

I had no wings, but He gave me the wings
to fly up high, to see from the top of the world.
Not to admire its greatness and beauty,
but to understand His Creation
and the beauty of our lives
when He puts them in order.

Time is short;
I must do what is good and right;
Not try to be great; but do what I can.

-- Physa Chanmany

"I thank the eternal God, my heavenly Father, who
has saved and preserved and strengthened my life."

Visit to Cambodia

Top right: (left to right) Physa, his cousin, his brother Boun and wife, a friend, and Physa's mother. In front, Boun's small daughter and the friend's two sons. At Angkor Thom, the 12th century fortified city built by a great Khmer king to honor Hindu gods. Bas reliefs depict colorful life in Medieval Cambodia among the peasants and the royal court, with elephant-mounted army.

Below: In front of wat Phnom, a Buddhist temple in Phnom Penh. Physa, second from left, and Boun, second from right, with friends, flanked by statues of the naga, seven-headed snake god. While a few people in the city are middle class (mostly leaders in military or government) Cambodians continue to suffer from the genocidal Khmer Rouge years. Most educated people and capable leaders were killed or driven out. Poverty, disease, and weakened family and village life; lack of medical care, education, books, and arts; as well as an unstable government leave Cambodia a blighted country. Healing for this stricken land seems humanly impossible. It will take God's love working through His people.

Below: In Rasopi, visiting friends from the old village of Kaubtom, who are working to build a new village on bare land. Visible here are planted banana trees, a chicken hut in rear, and a couple building a shelter for their pigs.

APPENDIX

Physa's Siblings

1. Boun -- The oldest child, ran away to Laos as a young man. Trained for the military in Russia, he became an officer in the Vietnamese Communist army that invaded Cambodia and took over the government from the Khmer Rouge, who were forced into hiding in the deep jungle along the Thai border. Retiring from the army in 1986, Boun continues to reside with his wife and child in Cambodia's capital, Phnom Penh.

2. Soon -- He married young in the home village. The family missed the first exodus to refugee camps in Thailand, because they waited for Soon's sick daughter (who died under the deprivations of the Khmer Rouge regime) and his lame father-in-law (who died after the second Communists took over). Soon and his family live in Cambodia, farming the plot of land given to them by the government, far from the original family village and without enough water to thrive. He is also a carpenter craftsman.

(3.) A boy, who died at age three of a fever, the only child Physa's mother has lost, out of eight children born to her.

3. Art -- He ran away from the village home as a youth, going to Laos and Thailand. The family lost

170

contact with Art and considered him the "lost brother" until Physa found him in San Francisco many years later. Married, he resides in California.

4. Naiang -- The first daughter, she escaped with her mother, sister and brother-in-law to Thailand in 1984. She was married in Thailand, where she now lives.

5. Nonglam -- Still living in Cambodia as a rice farmer and mechanic, he married in 1980 under the second Communist regime. When the Communists required their mother to send one of her two youngest sons into the army in 1979, Physa chose to go, so Nonglam, who was older and stronger, could continue farming and support their mother.

6. Physa (Tum) -- Assigned to patrol the dangerous and volatile Thai-Cambodian border, Physa escaped for his life and became separated from his family in 1979. He became a refugee to America in 1980, and a United States citizen in 1987. He returned to Cambodia and Thailand to visit his family in 1991 and 1997. He is now a Christian minister, living in Santa Rosa, California, where he married in 1997.

7. Pheny -- The youngest child, she married in Cambodia in 1982. She was pregnant when she escaped to Thailand with her husband, her mother, and her older sister, too late to be sent to America. The two sisters, their families, and their mother now live and farm in Thailand as Thai citizens.

BIBLIOGRAPHY

Jerry L. Appleby, *Missions Have Come to America* (Kansas City: Beacon Hill Press, 1986).

Eleanor G. Bowman, *Eyes Beyond the Horizon: Far East Broadcasting Company* (Nashville: Thomas Nelson, 1991).

David P. Chandler, *The Tragedy of Cambodian History--Politics, War and Revolution since 1945* (New Haven: Yale University Press, 1991).

Physa Chanmany, Video recordings filmed in Cambodia, personal and historical.

Don Cormack, *Killing Fields, Living Fields: An Unfinished Portrait of the Cambodian Church--the Church that Would Not Die* (Great Britain: Monarch Publications, 1997).

Sharon Sloan Fiffer, *Imagining America: Paul Thai's Journey From the Killing Fields of Cambodia to Freedom in the U.S.A.* (New York: Paragon House, 1991.

Goldcrest Films, *The Killing Fields* (Burbank: Warner Home Video, 1986).

Michael Freeman and Roger Warner, *ANGKOR: The Hidden Glories* (Boston: Houghton Mifflin, 1990)

Henry Kamm, *Cambodia: Report From A Stricken Land* (New York: Arcade Publishing, 1998)

Laos, A Country Study (Federal Research Division, Library of Congress, 1995).

Sydney H.Schanberg, *The Death and Life of Dith Pran* (New York: Viking, 1985).

Chris Taylor, *Cambodia: Travel Survival Kit* (Oakland: Lonely Planet, 1996).

Usha Welaratna, *Beyond the Killing Fields: Voices of Nine Cambodian Survivors in America* (Stanford University Press, 1993).

INTERNET:

Cambodia Web (General, up-to-date information on Cambodia) http:www.cambodia-web.net/index.htm

http://rossuk.simplenet.com/Cambodia (photos)

http://www.khmernet.com

Southeast Asian Outreach: The Cambodian Church, http://www.sao-cambodia.org/church.htm

To order additional copies of this book,
send $12.95 plus $2.50 shipping and
handling (California residents add 7.25%
sales tax) check or money order to:

CLADACH PUBLISHING
P.O. Box 355
Fulton, CA 95439

phone/fax: (707) 528-3128

Quantity discounts available.
Ask for a free catalog.

Visit our web site at:
http://www.cladach.com